TSAO YU

SUNRISE

A Play in Four Acts

by **TSAO YU**

Foreign Languages Press
Peking 1960

Translated by

A. C. BARNES

Printed in the People's Republic of China

PUBLISHER'S NOTE

Sunrise is a four-act play written by the famous contemporary Chinese playwright Tsao Yu in 1935. His first play, *Thunderstorm,* written in 1933, was published in English and French by our press in 1958. *Sunrise,* the author's second play, describes the dark life of the Chinese people during the period from 1931 to 1935 under the reactionary rule of the Kuomintang. For more than twenty years the play has been widely acclaimed. It is regarded as one of the outstanding works of the new Chinese literature which came into being after the May 4 Movement in 1919. The present translation is based on the first edition published by the Chinese Drama Press in Peking in 1957. The preface by Ouyang Shan-tsun gives a brief introduction to, and analysis of, the play.

"Nature's way is like an archer drawing a bow — making the top bend downwards and the bottom bend upwards — for it lops abundance and supplements need. This is Nature's way, but Man's way is quite otherwise: Man's way is to despoil the needy to enrich those who have more than enough."

— Chapter 77, Laotse's *Tao Te Ching*

Preface

by Ouyang Shan-tsun [1]

The author of *Sunrise*, Tsao Yu, was born into a family of feudal bureaucrats but came in contact with progressive ideas during his higher education. In 1933, when his days at university were almost at an end, he completed his maiden work, the four-act family tragedy *Thunderstorm*, through the medium of which he announced his rebellion against the kind of family from which he had come. After leaving university he stepped into the grotesque hurly-burly of the society of the time, where the nightmarish hideousness of human conduct filled him with an acute sense of discontentment and where injustice and cruelty stabbed into his heart like a sharp blade. He was painfully conscious of the darkness of the society in which he lived and he thirsted for sunlight, for springtime, for a decent life filled with happiness and laughter. This prompted him in 1935, in a mood of indignation and with intense feeling, to write his second play *Sunrise*. Through this play he cried aloud to the shameless reprobates who were ruling the dark society of that time: "Your last day is at hand!"

Sunrise was written in 1935 but the period it reflects is from 1931 to 1935. Ever since the failure of the First Revolutionary Civil War in 1927 the Chinese people had been living in the greatest misery under the infamous regime of the Kuomintang and Chiang Kai-shek, who

---

[1] Ouyang Shan-tsun is Deputy Director of the Peking People's Art Theatre.

depended more completely on the imperialists than any previous reactionary regime. With China in the grip of imperialism and feudalism, the civil wars of the new warlords dragged on unceasingly as before; they exploited and oppressed the people with even greater cruelty and bestiality than the old warlords and they created even more serious unemployment among the workers and bankruptcy in the villages, thus aggravating even more the crisis of the Chinese nation. In 1929 the economic crisis began in the capitalist countries, an extremely severe and unprecedentedly protracted crisis which continued until 1933 before turning to a depression. It was during just this period that Japanese imperialism intensified its occupation and looting of China: the fall of the three northeastern provinces on September 18, 1931, the defeat of Chinese troops in the battle of Shanghai started on January 28, 1932, and the making of such traitorous agreements as the Shanghai Peace Agreement, the Tangku Agreement and the Ho-Umez Agreement. During just this period, too, China's economic crisis was daily becoming more severe, especially in such great maritime cities as Shanghai and Tientsin, both of which were hit by a slump in trade. With factories stopping work, banks closing through insolvency and property prices falling, most capitalists tried the hazardous road of speculation and plunged into transactions in government bonds on the stock exchange, with the result that bulls and bears appeared who specialized in manipulating the market in government bonds. It was in just such circumstances as these that Pan Yueh-ting in the play tried to avert by means of speculation the disaster that threatened his Ta Feng Bank, though with the result that he met with miserable failure through the machinations of Chin Pa. The pseudo-prosperity of the business of speculation at that time was an abnormality indicating that the national economy of semi-feudal, semi-colonial China was on the brink of bankruptcy.

Under the infamous regime of the Kuomintang and Chiang Kai-shek, not only did the sufferings of the working class become even more tragic, not only were the peasants forced into an existence where they were stricken with hunger and cold, but life also became more difficult for the urban petty bourgeoisie. Their burden was made immeasurably heavier by the increase in all kinds of taxes and levies. As the various sectors of the national economy came to the brink of bankruptcy professional people, young students and intellectuals also began to be hit by unemployment, interruption of studies, privations and setbacks. White terror reigned supreme. The oppression which they suffered ideologically was without precedent in history. So it was quite natural that they should want to find a way out of their difficulties and that they should have tendencies towards revolution. It is in such circumstances as these that Fang Ta-sheng comes out with the exclamation: "Together we can achieve something! We can fight the Mr. Chins!"

The author, Tsao Yu, is a man with a great understanding of the theatre and the stage, and a playwright who writes his plays for performance and for the audience. He regards his plays as written for the ordinary theatregoer, who for him constitutes the entire life of the theatre. He opposes the kind of playwriting that can only stand the test of reading but not the test of performance. So his plays are always tense and enthusiastic, seizing the attention of the audience immediately and making an audience watching one of his plays now excited, now alarmed, now in tears, now laughing through their tears as various things happen to the characters in the play and as the plot unfolds. Before writing *Sunrise* the author reviewed his experiences in writing the preceding play *Thunderstorm*, and tried to change his style of writing. He remembered the Chekhov plays that he had read, and it seemed to him that in these works there was not the least intrusion of flamboyance, not a scene that had an excessive emotional impact; their construction was quite ordinary, yet they held one enthralled. He was intoxicated by the profound subtlety of that master's style and he made up his mind to take this pre-eminent quality of it as his own guide; and this is what he did in fact do in *Sunrise*. Has this resulted in his losing his own individual artistic style? By no means. It is quite apparent that the author's own style retains its pristine freshness and clarity in *Sunrise* and his characteristic tension and enthusiasm are preserved as prominently as ever. Although the colours which he has applied to the canvas of *Sunrise* are no longer so predominantly primary as in *Thunderstorm*, he has nevertheless chosen once again the vivid, brilliant hues that are appropriate to his own individuality.

Generally speaking, the first act of a play is always in danger of lapsing into dreariness in its efforts to make the audience acquainted with the unfamiliar characters and plot, but *Sunrise* has avoided this all-too-easy fault, for at one fell swoop it brings the audience into the lives of the characters on the stage and into the events that take place there.

In the succeeding acts more characters appear and in every case their appearance is quite natural and their clear-cut personalities hold our attention the moment they come on the scene. Mrs. Ku with her pose of sentimentality that she imagines makes her so attractive; the dandified Hu Sze, "the most handsome boy in China"; Li Shih-ching, who is cunning, spiteful and cringing and yet has his pride; Mrs. Li, simple and sedate, gentle and kind; Huang Hsing-san, humble, weak and nervous; the desperado Black San, ferocious and malevolent; Little Shun-tze, who has sympathy for the weak but is unable to help them, much as he would like to; Hua Tsui-hsi, who has a heart of gold despite the hell she lives in. In addition to these there are also the characters who have already appeared in Act One: Chen Pai-lu, Fang Ta-sheng and the smooth-tongued Georgy Chang with his ostentatious display of foreign phrases; the sly, time-serving, bullying rogue Wang Fu-sheng; the Shrimp, timid and diminutive yet full of the spirit of resistance; and the shameless sensualist Pan Yueh-ting, plump and sleek from comfortable living. All these many and various notes go into the making of this magnificent and complex symphony.

In these succeeding acts, too, the writer's artistry brings one tense and moving scene after another before our eyes. In the scene where Li Shih-ching and Pan Yueh-ting pit their wits against each other we can hear the sound of two keen blades clashing together and see the sparks that fly from their impact. Poised on the edge of a yawning abyss, they are locked in mortal combat on a precariously swaying rock, and the outcome is that they perish together. Into this scene where they are struggling together the writer deliberately inserts two episodes: that of Huang Hsing-san being driven to poison his children and that of the death of Li Shih-ching's child. In this way he gives an added poignancy to the situation that has been developed, makes its contrasts even sharper, and intensifies the cruel hideousness of the atmosphere. The third act of the play takes us into one of the darkest corners of that dark society, where a number of "pitiful creatures" like Tsui-hsi are suffering physical and spiritual degradation and ill-treatment in a hell on earth. We see Tsui-hsi leaving the Shrimp who has been viciously beaten by Black San, and then we see the Shrimp alone, closing the door, bolting it, picking up a piece of rope, climbing on to a stool, tying the rope on to a beam, getting down again and moving in a daze, walking slowly up and down, then suddenly stopping and in a low voice sobbing out the word "Father"; she kneels down facing the rope and kowtows low three times, then stands up with a sigh, climbs up on to the stool, and puts her head through the noose. . . . I am convinced that when an audience witnesses this scene every heart will turn to lead and not a breath will be drawn, then, after a moment's silence, a single cry will burst in unison from the bottom of every heart: "She must be avenged!"

Sunrise contains a wide diversity of characters distinguished one from the other by differences of class, birth, profession, temperament, social position and education, so the language of each of them must also be distinctive. In this the author has been successful. The passages of biting dialogue between Pan Yueh-ting and Li Shih-ching are very successful: the alternation of thrust and parry and the way words and phrases are deliberately made to rebound trenchantly on the one who uses them give full expression to the virulence and wiliness of both of them and to the sharpness of the conflict. Georgy Chang's language is larded with foreign words, making us vividly conscious of his slave-mentality. What is equally distressing to our ears is the stream of grotesquely-applied vogue-words that Mrs. Ku rattles off. This way of speaking of hers conjures up in our minds the image of a bloated, nauseating woman.

It can be seen from *Sunrise* that the author already realized at that time that there could be hope and a future only for the working class and that they alone are the possessors of "light and vitality," yet he keeps these most important positive characters offstage. He did this at the cost of considerable mental pain and the reason he did it was that "owl-eyed monsters were watching closely by my side day and night" (author's postscript to the Chinese edition of *Sunrise*). The political environment of that time was such that he could not do otherwise. Since he could not bring these "symbolizers of the light" on to the open stage, he was reduced to bringing on a bridge that would lead the audience to the light, and this bridge was Fang Ta-sheng.

In the past many critics have considered Fang Ta-sheng to be a figure of fun and a fit butt for ridicule, and some producers and actors have treated him as a bookish, unpractical character and have made him seem lukewarm and ineffectual. This way of regarding him and producing him cannot be considered correct. Fang Ta-sheng should be a positive, active character who gradually comes to see the light and goes courageously towards it. It is through him that optimism and the elements of a positive approach are brought to the audience. Let us cast our eye over the development of this character in the course of the play as a whole.

When Fang Ta-sheng appears first of all in Act One his manner is that of a Romeo and he asks Chen Pai-lu to marry him. Pai-lu refuses but wants him to stay and have a look at the monstrous metropolis and the people around them. In Act Two he comes into contact with these shamelessly dissolute people and experiences a violent loathing and hatred for them, but in contrast to this he on the other hand feels deep sympathy for the insulted and ill-used Shrimp and gets on very well with her. At the end of this act, when he discovers that she has been abducted, he goes with courage and determination in pursuit of her.

In Act Three he goes to such places as the third-class "Brothel of Precious Harmony" in search of the Shrimp and when he sees the darkness and degradation of life in these places he keeps thinking: "Why must people be so cruel to one another?" and "I can't make out why you people allow a beast like this Chin to go on living." In Act Four he admits to Pai-lu that she was right in wanting him to stay and have a longer look at the place and he says: ". . . I should have a closer look at these creatures here. Now I've seen them as they really are. . . . I may do a bit of work here. . . . I may have some dealings with Mr. Chin, I may run around looking for the Shrimp, or I may do something for people like that bank-clerk. I don't really know yet. I just feel there's a lot that could be done." Finally, when he hears the solemn, stirring voices of the labourers at their work, he says: "Listen! The sun is shining, the sun is on their faces. Come with me, together we can achieve something. We can fight the Mr. Chins!" And then he goes out with his head held high and the light of the sun on his face. He is far from being a man who has a high degree of political consciousness right from the start, he is not a revolutionary and even less is he a Communist; he is just a very ordinary young intellectual, and in many respects very immature, even: his view of labour, for example, is rather primitive and he has not been able to distinguish between the workers' conscious labour as their own masters and their labour under exploitation and oppression. But not only does this not in any way affect his positive role in the play, indeed it rather makes this character even more real and credible and hence more convincing. Communists, after all, are in a minority, but in old China there were many people like Fang Ta-sheng and if even people like him wanted to go and "fight the Mr. Chins" it shows how insecure the social system that supported the Mr. Chins had already become. The author makes Fang Ta-sheng lead us unconsciously to where we burst in upon a world of "sunrise"; with him we hate Chin Pa, Black San and Wang Fu-sheng, and with him we loathe Pan Yueh-ting, Georgy Chang, Mrs. Ku, Hu Sze and the rest of them; we are made to join with him in his sympathy for Pai-lu, the Shrimp, Huang Hsing-san, Hua Tsui-hsi and others of their kind and in his eventual realization that we ought to "fight the Mr. Chins."

The overall atmosphere of *Sunrise* is one of tension, jarring and restless anxiety, like the feeling of closeness and irritability that herald the approach of a storm in summer, and this is an exact reflection of the political atmosphere in that period of China's history. The political situation at that time was that various contradictions were rapidly developing and becoming more acute both at home and abroad, with the scourge of war extending its range day by day and the whole country in the grip of calamity, with the result that the masses of the workers and peasants and the poor of the cities were set on a road that could only lead to destruction. The whole of China, menaced by impending disaster, was in a state of turmoil and confusion, and anyone with a sense of justice would have realized that things could not go on like this and that a way must be found to change this state of affairs. In all this lay the explanation of the fact that a new high tide of revolution was due to arrive very soon. The atmosphere conveyed in *Sunrise* is the atmosphere of the eve of a new high tide of revolution.

The time-distribution of *Sunrise* is: dawn, dusk, midnight and sunrise. These are precisely the times when night and day, darkness and light, give way to one another.

The settings of *Sunrise* are a luxuriously-furnished sitting-room in a large hotel and a grimy room in a third-class brothel. On the surface these two places are very different, yet in essence they are very much alike. The occupants of these two rooms, Chen Pai-lu and Hua Tsui-hsi, are both women who are being subjected to degradation and ill-treatment in a perverted society, both selling their bodies, the only difference between them being that Chen Pai-lu charges a higher price for her body than Hua Tsui-hsi charges for hers. Chen Pai-lu's customers tend to be more "cultured" and more fastidious in their dress and to have more money in their pockets while Hua Tsui-hsi's customers tend to be more coarse and unprepossessing and to have less money in their pockets. And that is all. Through the actions of such typical characters at such a typical time in such typical places, the writer unrolls for us an immense painting of a cannibalistic society and as the painting unrolls we see that society crumbling and collapsing and we can smell the stench of decay and hear the sound of its crashing masonry.

In his postscript to the Chinese edition of *Sunrise* the author has said: "Some people after reading *Sunrise* may be prepared to ask indignantly why so many people should have to lead such a horrible existence. Surely we are not obliged to preserve such a world? What is the cause that has produced this world of injustice and barbarity? Should this system be reformed or completely overthrown? If there are people who really are prepared to ask a few such questions, that in itself would be beyond a writer's wildest dreams." These words were written more than twenty years ago and today, over twenty years later, the state of affairs depicted in *Sunrise* is already ancient history so far as the Chinese people are concerned. Led by the Communist Party of China, the Chinese people are working in bright sunshine building their own happy life.

Peking, October 5, 1958

THE CHARACTERS

CHEN PAI-LU, a woman living in the X Hotel, 23.

FANG TA-SHENG, Chen Pai-lu's erstwhile "friend," 25.

"GEORGY" CHANG, a man who has been a student in Europe, 31.

WANG FU-SHENG, a waiter in the hotel.

PAN YUEH-TING, manager of the Ta Feng Bank, 54.

MRS. KU, a wealthy widow, 44.

LI SHIH-CHING, secretary in the Ta Feng Bank, 42.

MRS. LI, his wife, 34.

HUANG HSING-SAN, a minor clerk in the Ta Feng Bank.

BLACK SAN, a gangster, the Shrimp's "father."

HU SZE, an idle, frivolous gigolo, 27.

THE SHRIMP, a girl of 15 or 16 who has not long been in the city.

THE CHARACTERS APPEARING
IN ACT III

TSUI-HSI, an old prostitute of about 30.

LITTLE SHUN-TZE, an attendant in the "Precious Harmony," a third-class brothel.

THE SHRIMP (LITTLE TSUI), a girl who has been in the business three days.

A PAPER-BOY, who is dumb.

WANG FU-SHENG.

HU SZE.

BLACK SAN.

FANG TA-SHENG.

Characters Offstage

A fat man and his friends.

An itinerant gramophone-player.

A paper-boy.

A fruit-seller and other hawkers of various other food-stuffs.

A crying infant.

A street-singer and a man who accompanies her on the two-stringed fiddle.

An attendant who announces the girls' names.

Two minstrel-beggars (singers of *shulaipao*).

A wandering singer of Peking opera.

A watchman beating a wooden gong.

Men and women making merry.

A shortbread seller.

A customer singing "You called me your little sweetheart" before the curtain falls.

A woman weeping softly.

TIME AND PLACE

ACT I Half past five one morning in early spring. The luxuriously-furnished sitting-room of a suite in X Hotel.

ACT II The same at five in the afternoon.

ACT III A third-class brothel, a week later at about twelve o'clock in the evening.

ACT IV The same as Act I, at about four o'clock the next morning.

Stage setting for Act I

Stage setting for Act III

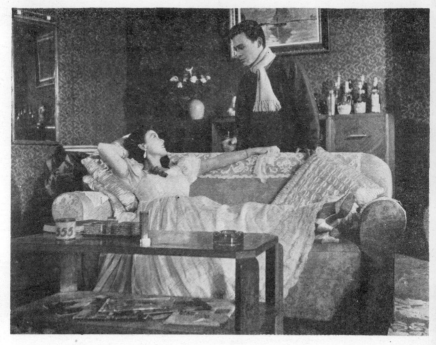

Ta-sheng: If only you'd come with me you could be as happy and free as you ever were. (Act I)

Black San: But look, we found a handkerchief that she'd dropped outside your door. (Act I)

Pai-lu: . . . The sun is risen. . . . (Act I)

Georgy: Tell them in the next room that I won't be joining them for mahjong. (Act II)

Black San: Here you are, sir, this
must be your girl-friend. (Act III)

Hu Sze: See this? I'm not short of money. (Act III)

Li: Then it appears, sir, that you're not prepared to keep your word to me. (Act IV)

Act I

The luxuriously-furnished sitting-room of a suite in
the X Hotel. In the centre a door opening on to a passage; on the right (i.e. actors' right, so audience' left) a
door leading to the bedroom; on the left another leading
to the reception-room. Let into the back wall, towards
the right-hand corner, is a large oblong window with a
rounded top. Tall buildings cluster tightly round the
outside of the window, so that even in the daytime the
room is overdark, despite the window's generous pro-
portions. Except for a slight brightening of the room
when the slanting rays of the sun find their way in in
the morning, not a gleam of natural light is visible all day
long.

The room is decorated and furnished throughout in a
bizarre, modernistic style whose superficiality and forced
effects arouse one's curiosity but give one absolutely no
feeling of restfulness. In the centre stands a small table
with ash-trays, cigarettes and so on, and strewn around
it is an array of arm-chairs and stools of various shapes
— square, round, cube-shaped, conical. Scattered over
these are chaotically-coloured cushions. Along the wall
under the cornerless window is a moire sofa. On the left
are a wardrobe, a food cupboard and a small table on
which are a number of women's cosmetics placed there
for immediate use. On the walls are several garish nudes,
a calendar and a copy of the hotel regulations. The floor
is littered with newspapers, illustrated magazines, bottles
and cigarette-ends. Various articles of feminine attire
— hats, scarves, gloves and so on — lie about on the
chairs and the top of the wardrobe. Among them is the

1

occasional male garment. The top of the food cupboard
is a welter of bottles, glasses, thermos flasks and teacups.
In the right-hand corner stands a reading-lamp, and
beside it is a small round table consisting of one glass
shelf above another and holding ash-trays and the kind
of knick-knacks that women are fond of, among them a
European doll and a Mickey Mouse.

In the centre of the back wall is a shining silver-
coloured clock which is now at half past five, the time
when darkness has almost left the sky. When the curtain
rises the only illumination is a pool of light from the
reading-lamp by the sofa. Yellow curtains are drawn
over the window, so that the details of the arrangement
of the room are not yet clearly discernible.

Leisurely footsteps approach along the passage. The
centre door creaks half-open. Chen Pai-lu comes in and
switches on the ceiling-light in the centre, filling the
room with a sudden blaze of light. She is dressed in an
extremely smart evening gown of gay colours; its many-
pleated skirt and the two long pink ribbons attached to
it trail behind her like a diaphanous cloud. She wears
a red flower in her jet-black hair, which has been waved
into two loose buns that resemble those of a little girl
and fall over her ears. Her eyes are bright and attractive,
her movements are dainty and alert, and a mocking smile
is always on her lips. But her expression from time to
time betrays weariness and distaste; this weariness of
life is a characteristic of rootless women like her. She
loves life, but she also detests it. She has come to realize
that the ways of life she has become accustomed to are
the cruelest of shackles and, however much she may
long for freedom, these shackles will always prevent her
from escaping from the net of her environment. She has
tried several times to escape, but in the end, like the pro-
verbial bird that has become so accustomed to its gilded
cage that it has lost the ability and the desire to fly in
freedom among the trees, she has each time returned to

*the sordid confines of the life she had left, though with
the greatest of reluctance.*

*She now moves with weary, dragging steps to the
centre of the stage. She yawns, covering her mouth with
her right hand.*

CHEN PAI-LU (*looking back towards the door after a few
steps*): Come on in! (*She tosses her bag down and leans
against the back of the sofa in the middle of the room.
Frowning, she takes off her high-heeled silver shoes
and gently massages her slender feet with evident re-
lief. Now that she is home at long last there's nothing
for it but to flop down on a soft sofa and relax. Suddenly, she realizes that the person behind her has not followed her in. Slipping on her shoes, she jumps up and
turns round with one leg still kneeling on the sofa and
smile towards the door.*) I say, why don't you come
in?
(*Now, someone does come in — Fang Ta-sheng. He is
about twenty-seven or eight years old, frowning
disagreeably and dressed in a European overcoat which
shows signs of wear. Looking in on the disordered state
of the room, he stands in the doorway without uttering
a word, though whether on account of tiredness or of
distaste is not clear. But Pai-lu misinterprets his hes-
itation and as she stares intently at him she thinks she
detects an expression of alarm and suspicion.*)
PAI-LU: Come right in. What are you afraid of?
FANG TA-SHENG (*calmly*): I'm not afraid of anything.
(*Suddenly uneasy*) There's nobody in here, is there?
PAI-LU (*looking all round, teasing him*): Who knows?
(*Looking across at him*) No, probably not.
TA-SHENG (*with distaste*): Sickening. Can't get away
from people in this place.
PAI-LU (*trying to unsettle him, and also of course be-
cause his attitude annoys her*): Anyway, what if there

were anyone here? You can't very well fight shy of people while you're in this place!

TA-SHENG (*looking across at her, then looking around him*): So this is where you've been living all these years.

PAI-LU (*challengingly*): What do you mean, is there something wrong with it?

TA-SHENG (*slowly*): Um — (*feeling that he has no alternative*) no, no, it's all right.

PAI-LU (*smiling at the nonplussed way he just stands and stares*): Why don't you take your things off?

TA-SHENG (*suddenly taking a hold of himself*): Oh, er, — my things? (*Unable to think of a suitable reply*) No, I haven't, I haven't taken them off.

PAI-LU (*amused at his manner*): I know you haven't. What I mean is, why are you being so formal that you won't even take your overcoat off without being asked?

TA-SHENG (*unable to find an explanation to offer, somewhat embarrassed*): Er — don't you find it a bit chilly in here?

PAI-LU: *Chilly,* you say? It seems very hot to me.

TA-SHENG (*seeking to distract her attention from himself*): Perhaps you didn't close the window properly, could that be it?

PAI-LU (*shaking her head*): Couldn't be. (*She goes over and pulls back the curtains to reveal the window with its streamlined frame.*) Look, it's shut tight. (*With sudden delight as she looks out of the window*) I say, look! Come and look!

TA-SHENG (*going across hurriedly, not knowing what she means*): What is it?

PAI-LU (*drawing her finger across the glass*): Look, frost! Frost! It's odd, having frost when spring's already here.

TA-SHENG (*giving up*): Yes, very odd.

PAI-LU (*elatedly*): I love frost! Remember how I liked it when I was little? Isn't it beautiful, really lovely!

(*Pointing suddenly, like a child*) Look, look at that, isn't that me?

TA-SHENG: Eh? (*Craning forward*) Who?

PAI-LU (*pointing excitedly at the window*): I mean the frost on the window, this bit. (*Annoyingly, he looks at the wrong place.*)   No, this bit. Look, isn't that two eyes? This sticking out is a nose, and where it goes in there is a mouth, and this patch is the hair. (*Clapping her hands*) Look at the hair, isn't it me exactly?

TA-SHENG (*like a blind man*):   I can't see that it's like you.

PAI-LU (*downcast*):   Oh, you! You're still as pigheaded as ever.   You're impossible.

TA-SHENG: Am I? (*With a sudden smile*) I've been looking at you all night but just now was the first time you've been like you used to be.

PAI-LU: What do you mean?

TA-SHENG (*an expression of happiness coming into his face*):   You're still the little girl that you used to be.

PAI-LU (*her high spirits of a moment ago suddenly pass away like a breath of wind. She sighs and says as if broken by age*): Was there once a time when I was like that, Ta-sheng?   Was I really a happy little girl once?

TA-SHENG (*understanding her state of mind, encouragingly*):   If only you'd come with me you could be as happy and free as you ever were.

PAI-LU (*shaking her head, in the voice of one who has long experienced the hard knocks of life*): Humph, where is there any freedom?

TA-SHENG: You — (*He looks at her and thinks better of it. He walks up and down a few steps then stops and looks about him.*)

PAI-LU (*having now recovered her accustomed air of detachment*):   What are you looking at now?

TA-SHENG (*with a brief smile*):   This place you've got here, it's quite nice.

PAI-LU (*she realizes what is in his mind but does not think it worth making excuses. She casually picks up a cushion that is lying at her feet and drops it on the sofa, at the same time kicking under the sofa an empty wine-bottle that has been left lying on the floor. She says offhandedly*): Somewhere to live, it's good enough for that. (*She yawns involuntarily.*) Tired?

TA-SHENG: No, I'm all right. — I was sitting down all the time while you were dancing with those people.

PAI-LU: Why didn't you join in the fun?

TA-SHENG (*coolly*): I don't dance, and these friends of yours looked mad to me, every one of them.

PAI-LU (*with a slightly unnatural laugh*): Mad's the word! That's the sort of mad life I lead, day in, day out. (*The crowing of a cock is heard in the distance.*) There's a cock crowing already.

TA-SHENG: That's odd, hearing a cock crow in a place like this.

PAI-LU: There's a market quite near. (*Glancing at her watch and looking sharply up again*) Guess what the time is.

TA-SHENG (*concentrating with an effort*): Must be about half past five, it'll be light soon. I was looking at my watch every five minutes at that dance-hall.

PAI-LU (*mockingly*): You *must* have been in a state!

TA-SHENG (*frankly*): You know I've been living down in the country for a long time now; I always get impatient in a noisy, crowded place like that.

PAI-LU (*doing her hair*): And now?

TA-SHENG (*sighing*): I feel more at my ease now, of course. I thought that since we'd be alone here I could have a word with you.

PAI-LU: Yes, but (*yawning again, her hand over her mouth*) it's almost morning. (*Suddenly*) Here, why don't you sit down?

TA-SHENG (*formally*): You — you haven't sat down yet.

PAI-LU (*laughing and showing her even white teeth*): You *are* old-fashioned. None of my friends that come to see me here ever wait to be asked before they sit down! (*Going across to him and gently pushing him on to an arm-chair*) Sit down. (*Turning and going over to the sideboard*) I'm parched, so I hope you'll excuse me for a moment while I have a drink of water. (*Pouring a glass of water and picking up a cigarette-box*) Smoke?

TA-SHENG (*staring at her*): I told you just a moment ago that I don't smoke.

PAI-LU (*good-humouredly mocking him*): You *are* a paragon of virtue! (*She deftly lights a cigarette and exhales a leisurely plume of pale-blue smoke.*)

TA-SHENG (*as he watches her skilfully blow a smoke-ring a sudden sigh escapes his lips and he says sadly and sympathetically*): I never expected, Chu-chun, that you'd change —

PAI-LU (*putting down her cigarette*): Wait a minute, what did you call me?

TA-SHENG (*taken aback*): Your name, don't you like hearing it or something?

PAI-LU (*nostalgically*): Chu-chun, Chu-chun, it seems years since anyone called me that.

TA-SHENG (*as if in pain*): When I see what you're like now, I — if only you knew how my heart —

(*He stops as a man emerges unsteadily from the bed-room on the right; he is in evening dress with his stiff collar askew. As he sways and staggers one of his sleeves, which is hanging loose, swings backwards and forwards. Pai-lu and Ta-sheng look round together to find their visitor standing quite unabashed in the doorway with one hand raised to support himself on the door-post, his face red and his hair hanging down in wisps. Perched on the end of his nose is a pair of platinum spectacles and he shows the whites of his eyes as he stares over the top of them, hiccuping with a sound like the lowing of a cow. It is Chang Chiao-chih.)*

THE VISITOR (*in a low, mysterious voice*): Sh! (*He adjusts his spectacles and points with an erratically moving finger.*)

PAI-LU (*startled*): Georgy!

GEORGY (*waving his hand, even more mysteriously*): Sh! (*He reels across to Ta-sheng and says in a low voice.*) What did you say? (*Pointing a finger at him*) What was that about? (*Turning familiarly to Pai-lu*) Who is this, Pai-lu?

TA-SHENG (*displeased but not knowing quite what to do*): Who is he, Chu-chun? Who is this man?

GEORGY (*as if to himself*): Chu-chun? (*To Ta-sheng*) You've made a mistake, her name's Pai-lu. She's our idol here, the queen of them all, the girl I — the girl I adore most of all!

PAI-LU (*exasperated*): You're drunk!

GEORGY (*pointing to himself*): Me? (*Shaking his head*) I'm not drunk! (*Pointing with an unsteady hand at Pai-lu*) It's you who're drunk! (*Pointing at Ta-sheng*) And you! (*As Ta-sheng turns his head towards him from looking at Pai-lu his face shows even greater contempt, but their visitor is now directing his remarks at him alone.*) Just look at you, look at the way you just sit and stare, so drunk that you don't know whether you're coming or going! Oh, I've no patience with you. (*He hiccups once again.*)

PAI-LU (*really losing patience with him*): What are you doing here, anyway?

TA-SHENG (*more sure of himself now*): Yes, what *are* you doing here? (*He fixes Georgy with a look of interrogation.*)

GEORGY (*his mind fuddled by drink*): I—er—I was tired, I wanted to go to sleep. (*As a point suddenly occurs to him*) But wait, you're both here, too!

PAI-LU: This is where I live, so of course I'm here!

GEORGY (*dubiously*): Where you live? Never!

PAI-LU (*becoming more annoyed still*): And what were you doing in my bedroom?

GEORGY: What! (*More incredulously than ever*) Me in your bedroom? But you're wrong, I wasn't (*shaking his head*), I wasn't. (*Patting his forehead*) Though let me just think. . . . (*He gazes upwards as if thinking.*)

PAI-LU (*looking across at Ta-sheng as if she does not know whether to laugh or cry*): He wants to think, he says!

GEORGY (*waving his hand at them as if telling them to calm down*): Easy does it, just give me time, don't rush me. Now, let me work things out, slowly, slowly. (*He now gropes through his memory, muttering to himself.*) And then I had a drink and everything went round, and afterwards I had another drink and everything went round again, round and round, round and round . . . and after that . . . I got into the lift . . . (*delightedly, patting his forehead*) then I came into this room, and then I felt sick and flopped down on the bed and — ugh! — (*patting his head and resuming his normal voice*) yes, that's what happened. Well, *of course*, I'm now out here!

PAI-LU (*sternly*): And now you can clear out!

GEORGY (*his forefinger on his lips, in the manner of a Hollywood film-star*): Sh! (*In a normal speaking voice*) Oh, damn, I'm going to be sick again. (*Holding his hand over his mouth*) Pardon me, excuse me! . . . Please forgive me! Goodbye. *Bonsoir! Bonsoir!* (*There is a sound of retching as he hurriedly covers his mouth and stumbles out of the room.*)

(*Pai-lu looks across at Ta-sheng then sits down resignedly.*)

TA-SHENG (*with more distaste than he can express in words*): Who was that?

PAI-LU (*sighing*): One of our choicer local products, don't you think he's rather fun?

TA-SHENG: I can't think what induces you to mix with such riff-raff.

PAI-LU (*her cigarette between her fingers*): You really want to know? He's the cream of our local products. He's studied abroad and says he's a Ph.D. or an M.A. or something. His European name is George, when he's abroad he calls himself George Chang and when he's in China he calls himself Chang Chiao-chih. Since he's been back he's apparently had several administrative posts, and he's made himself quite a nice little pile.

TA-SHENG (*going up to her*): How does that bring you into the picture?

PAI-LU (*tapping the ash from her cigarette*): Haven't I just told you? He's got money.

TA-SHENG: You mean that just because he's got money you. . . .

PAI-LU (*bluntly saying it for him*): If he's got money of course he can be an acquaintance of mine. When I was at the dance-hall he was running after me for quite some time.

TA-SHENG (*realizing that the woman in front of him is no longer what she used to be*): No wonder he behaved like that to you, then. (*He bows his head.*)

PAI-LU: You're a real countryman, so serious about everything. Wait till you've been here for a few days and you'll realize what living really means. Everyone behaves like that, you needn't be so priggish about it. Well, now, there's no one else here, so let's get back to what you wanted to talk to me about, eh?

TA-SHENG (*coming out of a reverie*): What was I saying to you?

PAI-LU: You've a shocking memory. (*Brightly*) You were telling me about your heart, weren't you? And then this Mr. Chang Chiao-chih arrived.

TA-SHENG (*sighing*): Yes, "my heart." I'm that sort of person, you see, who always lives by his heart. But Chu-chun (*earnestly*), when I see you like this, you cannot imagine how my heart — (*He stops as the door creaks open.*) Mr. Chang back again, I suppose.
(*Their visitor is Wang Fu-sheng, a waiter in the hotel, with a sly face and an obsequiously deferential manner.*)

FU-SHENG: No, it's not Mr. Chang, it's me. (*With an ingratiating smile*) You're back early, Miss Chen.

PAI-LU: Did you want to see me about something?

FU-SHENG: You saw Mr. Chang just now.

PAI-LU: Well, what about it?

FU-SHENG: I helped him along to another room and put him to bed.

PAI-LU (*annoyed*): He can go where he pleases. You don't have to come and tell me about it!

FU-SHENG: I know, but Mr. Chang says he's terribly sorry about getting drunk and coming into your suite and being sick on your bed, and —

PAI-LU: What! He's been sick on my bed?

FU-SHENG: Yes, but don't worry, Miss Chen, I'll clean it up for you at once. (*Pai-lu gets up but he bars her way.*) I'd rather you didn't go in yourself, it'll only upset you to see it.

PAI-LU: Oh, the beast, he — all right, then, you see to it.

FU-SHENG: Right. (*Pausing and turning as he moves away*) There have been quite a lot of visitors, but you've been out all night tonight. There's been Mr. Li, and Mr. Fang, and Mr. Liu. Mr. Pan the bank-manager came three times to see you. And then there was a phone call from Mrs. Ku saying could you go over to her place tomorrow — er, today, that is — to spend the evening with them.

PAI-LU: I see. You can give her a ring later on and ask her here for the afternoon.

FU-SHENG: And Mr. Hu said he'd be coming to see you soon.

PAI-LU: Tell him he can come if he wants to. Any and everyone's welcome here.

FU-SHENG: Then there was the newspaper-editor, Mr. Chang —

PAI-LU: Yes, yes, tell him to come over today if he's free.

FU-SHENG: Oh yes, and Mr. Pan looked in three times during the night, and now he's —

PAI-LU (*impatiently*): Yes, yes, you've told me once already.

FU-SHENG: But, Miss Chen, now that this gentleman here —

PAI-LU: Oh, that's all right, this gentleman's a cousin of mine.

TA-SHENG (*puzzled*): A cousin?

PAI-LU (*to Fu-sheng*): He'll be sleeping here in the hotel.

TA-SHENG: No, Chu-chun, I'm not, I'll be going soon.

PAI-LU: Very well, then (*put out by his unexpected obtuseness*), please yourself. (*To Fu-sheng*) That's all then. Now you can go and get my bed cleaned up. (*Fu-sheng goes into the bedroom.*)

TA-SHENG: Chu-chun, I never imagined you could have become so —

PAI-LU (*sharply*): So what?

TA-SHENG (*intimidated by her manner*): E — er — so hospitable, so open-handed.

PAI-LU: Haven't I always been open-handed?

TA-SHENG (*still beating about the bush*): Oh, I — I didn't mean it like that. . . . I mean, you seem much more broad-minded than you used to —

PAI-LU (*swiftly*): You can't say I was ever narrow-minded! Oh, come off it! You've no need to be so mealy-mouthed about it with me. I know what you're thinking: I'm rather too free and easy, too reckless.

You most probably have a suspicion that I'm quite
immoral, haven't you?

TA-SHENG (*with a sudden burst of courage*): Er — yes.
You have changed a lot. You're just not the girl I
used to think you were. The way you speak, the way
you walk, your whole attitude and actions, everything,
in fact. You've just changed completely. All night
I sat in the dance-hall watching you. You were no
longer the delightful unaffected little girl that you
used to be, you'd changed. I'm quite disappointed,
utterly disappointed.

PAI-LU (*feigning surprise*): Disappointed?

TA-SHENG (*miserably*): Yes, disappointed. I didn't
expect to come here and find you changed into such
an easy-going woman. I heard all sorts of things about
you when I was over a thousand miles away, but I
didn't believe them. I didn't believe that the girl that
I used to like best of all could give people cause to
speak of her as utterly worthless. So I come to see
you, and I find you living *here*. A single girl, living
alone in a hotel, making friends with a lot of dubious
characters — this way of going on is just — immoral,
decadent — what do you expect me to say?

PAI-LU (*standing up and putting on a show of being
extremely angry*): How dare you call me decadent!
How dare you say you're disappointed in me, to my
face! What is there between us that you dare preach
at me like this?

TA-SHENG: Well, of course, there's nothing between
us now.

PAI-LU (*not letting up*): Are you trying to make out
there ever was?

TA-SHENG (*faltering*): I — er — no, of course not, if
you put it like that. (*Looking at the floor*) Though
you should remember that you were very fond of me
once. Besides, you do know why I've come here to
see you.

PAI-LU (*stonily*): No, I don't. Why?

TA-SHENG (*pleadingly*): I do wish you wouldn't be like this, making out you don't understand. You know very well that it was because I want to take you back with me.

PAI-LU (*wide-eyed*): Take me back? Where to? You know quite well I've no family to go back to.

TA-SHENG: No, no, I mean go back to my place. You ought to start a home of your own.

PAI-LU (*as if suddenly understanding everything for the first time*): Oh, I see, you mean the reason you came and looked me up yesterday was that you were bringing me an offer of marriage from someone? (*In a tone of voice suggesting that she understands at last what it is all about*) A — a — ah!

TA-SHENG (*not to be shaken off*): I'm not asking you to marry someone else, I'm asking you to marry me. (*He takes out train-tickets.*) I've got the tickets here, all ready. If you do decide to come, we can catch the ten o'clock train in the morning and get away from this place without more ado.

PAI-LU: Let me look. (*Taking the tickets*) So you really have bought two, a return and a single — sleepers, too! (*Smiling*) You think of everything.

TA-SHENG (*nervously*): You do agree to it, then. That's that, then.

PAI-LU: No, wait a minute. I've got just one question to ask you —

TA-SHENG: What?

PAI-LU (*with calm dignity*): How much money have you?

TA-SHENG (*taken unawares*): I don't understand what you mean.

PAI-LU: No? I mean can you keep me.

(*Ta-sheng is too amazed to reply, since he has not been thinking in these terms.*)

PAI-LU: Now what? You needn't look at me like that! Don't you think I should speak about such things? Come now, surely you can understand my wanting someone to keep me? Don't you understand that I want to live comfortably? When I go out I'll want to go by car, and when I entertain I'll want nice things to wear, I'll want to have a good time, I'll want to spend money, lots and lots of money, surely you understand that?

TA-SHENG (coldly): Chu-chun, you've forgotten you've had an education, that you're a young lady from an intellectual family.

PAI-LU: Shall I tell you something else? I'm a leading light in society, I've been in films, and I've been a dancing-star.

TA-SHENG (disdainfully): You seem very pleased with yourself.

PAI-LU: Why shouldn't I be? I've made my own way in the world, without depending on family or friends, on my own to sink or swim. And here I am today, alive and kicking, as you can see for yourself, so why shouldn't I be pleased with myself?

TA-SHENG: But do you think the money you've made in this way is honourably come by?

PAI-LU: You poor innocent, do you imagine the money made by your "honourable people" is come by honourably, then? We've heaps of respectable people here, as you'll see, all sorts and conditions, bankers, business men, civil servants, the lot. If you think their professions are honourable ones, then the money I make in this way is far more honourably come by than theirs.

TA-SHENG: I don't quite see what you mean, though perhaps our ideas of what's honourable —

PAI-LU: Yes, perhaps you and I have slightly different ideas of what's honourable. I haven't intentionally hurt anyone, I haven't taken the food out of other people's mouths, I like money and I try to make money, the same as they do, but I get my money by sacrificing my most precious possession. I haven't schemed to swindle people, I haven't extorted money by trickery; I live by other people's willing support, because I've sacrificed myself. I've performed the most pitiful service that a woman can render a man, and I'm enjoying the privileges that a woman deserves to enjoy!

TA-SHENG (*looking into her shining eyes*): It's horrible, horrible — it seems impossible that you can now have become so unscrupulous, so devoid of any sense of shame. Sure you realize that once one's head is turned by a lust for money, the most precious thing in life — love — will fly away like a bird.

PAI-LU (*with a touch of sorrow*): Love? (*Tapping the ash off her cigarette, in a leisurely voice*) What is love? (*She blows the word away into nothingness in a curling wisp of cigarette smoke*) You're a child! I've nothing more to say to you.

TA-SHENG (*undaunted*): Now Chu-chun, it seems to me that the way you've been living these last few years has killed a part of you. But now that I've come here and seen how you're living I can't bear to see you going on in the same way any longer. I'm determined to convert you, I'm —

PAI-LU (*unable to restrain her mirth*): What! You want to convert me?

TA-SHENG: Go on, then, laugh; now it's my turn to stop trying to argue with you. I know you think I'm a fool, coming all this way to look for you and then coming out with all this nonsense. But I want to make one more request. I want to repeat that I'm hoping you'll agree to marry me; think it over carefully, because I want a satisfactory answer within twenty-four hours.

PAI-LU (*with an assumed expression of alarm*): Twenty-four hours? You terrify me. But supposing that when

the time's up you get an unsatisfactory answer, what
will you do then? Force me to marry you?

TA-SHENG: If you won't marry me —

PAI-LU: You'll do what?

TA-SHENG (*miserably*): I'll — I may kill myself.

PAI-LU: What! (*Annoyed*) So you've picked up that
dodge, too, have you?

TA-SHENG: No (*feeling he is being rather too fashionable in saying this*), no, I won't kill myself. Don't
worry, I won't kill myself on a woman's account; I'll
go away, as far away as I can.

PAI-LU (*putting down her cigarette*): There now, now
you're speaking like an adult. (*Standing up*) Well,
my silly boy, there's no need for you to wait twenty-
four hours: I won't marry you, under any circumstances whatever.

TA-SHENG: Why — why not?

PAI-LU: For no reason at all! You really are impossible! One just can't find reasons for this kind of
thing. Surely you understand that?

TA-SHENG: Then I don't mean anything to you?

PAI-LU: You could put it that way, I suppose. (*Ta-
sheng tries to grasp her hand but she moves nimbly
and gracefully over to the wall.*)

TA-SHENG (*looking across at her and sinking brokenly
on to the arm-chair*): Was that what you really feel,
what you said just now? Weren't you even slightly
carried away by your emotions?

PAI-LU: Do I still look the sort of person to be carried
away by emotion after all this time?

TA-SHENG (*standing up again*): Chu-chun! (*He picks
up his hat.*)

PAI-LU: What are you doing now?

TA-SHENG: We must say good-bye now.

PAI-LU: Yes, good-bye. (*Taking his hand, with exaggerated sorrow*) So it's good-bye for always, then.

TA-SHENG (*broken-heartedly*): Yes, for always.

PAI-LU (*watching him to the door*):   You're really going?

TA-SHENG (*like a child*):   Yes.

PAI-LU: I suppose you've forgotten your return ticket, then.

TA-SHENG: Oh!   (*He comes back.*)

PAI-LU (*holding up the tickets*):   You're really going?

TA-SHENG (*looking up*):   Why?

PAI-LU: Aren't these your tickets?

TA-SHENG: Yes, what about it?

PAI-LU: Now watch, once like this (*tearing the tickets in two*) and then like this (*tearing them in four and throwing them into a spittoon*), I'll keep them in there for you.   All right?

TA-SHENG: You — why have you —

PAI-LU: Don't you understand?

TA-SHENG (*hope dawning in his face*):   So you've accepted me after all, then, Chu-chun?

PAI-LU: No, no, you've misunderstood, I haven't accepted you.   When I tore up your tickets I wasn't tearing up my own contract of sale.   I'm sold to this place for life.

TA-SHENG: Then why won't you let me go?

PAI-LU (*earnestly*):   Do you think you're the only person in the world with feelings?   Surely my not being able to marry you doesn't mean that I have to hate you, does it?   Haven't you even enough affection left for me to spend a couple of days with me and talk over old times?   You're so old-fashioned.   Can't we be good friends without getting married?   Surely something remains of the feelings we use to have for one another, something we'd like to share for a while?   As soon as you get inside the door you begin looking askance at me, disapproving of everything.   You say it's wrong of me to do this and wrong of me to do that.   You read me a lecture, you call me names, you thoroughly despise me, and then you demand that I marry you at once.   *And* you demand an answer within twenty-four

hours, and then you want me to go away with you
immediately.

TA-SHENG (*woodenly*): That's the way I've always
been; I'm no good at declarations of love. If you
want me to make pretty speeches, well, I just can't
do it.

PAI-LU: All right, then, so it won't hurt you to get
some more practice in with me; in a few days you
will be able to do it. Well, now, do you want to spend
a couple of days talking with me?

TA-SHENG (*bluntly*): But what about?

PAI-LU: Oh, there are heaps of things to talk about.
I can show you all round the city and entertain you
in style, and you can see how the people here live.

TA-SHENG: No, don't bother, the people here give me
the creeps. I don't need to see them. And anyway,
my luggage was sent to the station yesterday.

PAI-LU: Has it *really* been sent to the station?

TA-SHENG: Why, you know I never — never tell lies.

PAI-LU: Fu-sheng.

(*The waiter comes out of the bedroom.*)

FU-SHENG: Don't worry, Miss Chen, I'll have your
bed all tidied up right away.

PAI-LU: The luggage I told you to fetch from the Orient
Hotel when I went out: did you bring it?

FU-SHENG: You mean Mr. Fang's, yes I've brought it.
I fetched it from the hotel.

TA-SHENG: How dare you remove my luggage just as
you think you will, Chu-chun!

PAI-LU: Well, there it is, I did dare remove it from
your hotel. So much for your never telling lies, you
numskull. (*To Fu-sheng*) Which suite have you put
it in?

FU-SHENG: Number 24, East Wing.

PAI-LU: Is it the best suite?

FU-SHENG: The best in the hotel apart from this one
of yours.

PAI-LU: Good. Will you show Mr. Fang to his suite, then? If it's not to Mr. Fang's liking, tell me, and he can have mine.

FU-SHENG: Very good, Miss Chen. (*He goes out.*)

TA-SHENG (*colouring*): But Chu-chun, this is hardly respectable —

PAI-LU: There are a lot of things in this city that are hardly respectable. Now that you're here I'm inviting you to have a look round, so that you can get rid of some of your old-fashioned narrow-mindedness. When you've seen something more of it you'll realize that it is respectable.

TA-SHENG: No, Chu-chun, this needs thinking about.

PAI-LU: Now stop talking nonsense. Off you go! (*Pushing him*) Fu-sheng, Fu-sheng, Fu-sheng!
(*Fu-sheng comes in.*)

TA-SHENG: I could *never* sleep in a hotel like this.

PAI-LU: If you can't sleep I've got some sleeping-tablets here; a couple of these and you'll sleep through any amount of noise. You want some?

TA-SHENG: Stop playing about, I tell you I don't want to look at the place.

PAI-LU: Yes, you must, I insist that you have a look at it. (*To Fu-sheng*) Take him along to see his suite. (*Pushing Ta-sheng as she speaks*) Now hurry up and have a bath and get some sleep in. When you get up, put on some fresh clothes and I'll take you out. Now come along, there's a good boy, do as you're told. D'you hear? Good night — (*a cock crows in the distance*) listen, it really is getting late. Now come along, off to bed.
(*Ta-sheng reluctantly allows himself to be pushed out of the room. Fu-sheng follows him out.*)
(*She closes the door and leans against the door-post for a moment. A night of drinking and smoking and excitement has drained away much of her energy. She yawns, goes over to the table and lights a cigarette.*

A cock crows in the distance. Outside the window a deep blue is gradually penetrating the darkness. She throws away her cigarette and goes lightly and swiftly to the window. She switches off the light and opens the window. The outlines of the buildings outside gradually begin to show in the grey light that comes before the dawn. She leans out of the window and greedily inhales the cool air of early morning.)

(From the distance comes the sound of a factory hooter. It is still dark inside the room. A figure now steals silently out from behind the food-cupboard on the left and stands up holding on to the cupboard, trembling, then tiptoes towards the door, preparing to take this opportunity to slip away. Pai-lu now becomes aware of a stealthy noise behind her. She at once turns round. The figure stays rooted to the spot, quite immobile.)

PAI-LU *(in a low voice)*: Who's there? *(No reply. She is benumbed with fright.)* Who is it? Who are you? *(Still no reply. She raises her voice.)* What are you doing here?

THE FIGURE *(holding her breath)*: I . . . I . . . .

(Pai-lu slips quickly over to the light-switch and presses it, flooding the room with a blaze of light. Standing before her is a frail, timid girl, apparently about fifteen or sixteen years old, two small plaits hanging down over her chest and her hair in disorder, staring at Pai-lu in wide-eyed alarm, her cheeks stained by two rivulets of tears. She is wearing a blue silk coat, spattered with grease-stains and much too big for her, its bottom and sleeves almost trailing on the floor. The trousers beneath it are also immense, and the bottoms of the legs are dragging on the floor around her feet. This ensemble makes her look extremely timid and minute, like a baby wrapped round with adult garments. She is trembling pitifully with cold and terror, and her bright, clear eyes are innocent and imploring.

Her head bent, she shuffles backwards inch by inch, nervously holding up the legs of her trousers with her hands, afraid she will trip over them if she is not very careful.)

PAI-LU (*looking at the comical yet pitiful creature*): Why, you're only a little shrimp after all.

THE SHRIMP (*fearful and shamefaced*): Yes, Miss. (*She hobbles backwards step by step until, not careful enough, she treads on a trouser-leg and almost trips over.*)

PAI-LU (*finding it difficult not to laugh, but managing to keep a straight face*): Well, and what are you doing here, stealing? Eh?

THE SHRIMP (*nervously fingering her coat*): No, I — I'm not stealing.

PAI-LU (*pointing*): Then whose are these clothes you've got on?

THE SHRIMP (*looking down and examining her clothes*): My — my mother's.

PAI-LU: And who's your mother?

THE SHRIMP (*giving Pai-lu a look and absent-mindedly brushing a wisp of hair out of her eyes*): My mother? — I don't know who my mother is.

PAI-LU (*smiling, but still sizing her up*): Why, you silly girl, you must know who your mother is, surely! Where does your mother live?

THE SHRIMP (*pointing to the ceiling*): Upstairs.

PAI-LU: Upstairs. (*Suddenly understanding*) Oh, so you're from upstairs. You poor thing. How did you manage to get away?

THE SHRIMP (*her voice so low as to be almost inaudible*): I — I wanted to get away.

PAI-LU: Why?

(*The Shrimp bends her head and makes no reply.*)

PAI-LU: What was the matter?

THE SHRIMP (*hesitantly*): The night before last they — (*Fear prevents her from continuing.*)

PAI-LU: Come on, tell me, you needn't be afraid to speak here.

THE SHRIMP: The night before last they wanted me to sleep with a dark fat man. I was terrified, and I wouldn't, so they — (*She sobs.*)

PAI-LU: They beat you.

THE SHRIMP (*nodding*). Yes, with a whip. Last night they brought me here again and the dark fat man came again. I was really terrified of him. I was so frightened that I started shouting, and then the dark fat man went off in a rage and they — (*She sobs.*)

PAI-LU: They beat you again.

THE SHRIMP (*shaking her head, tearfully*): No, there was someone in the next room and they were afraid they might hear. They put a gag in my mouth, pinched me, and (*bursting into tears*) . . . and . . . and stuck opium-needles in me (*holding back her tears*), look, look! (*She holds out her arm and Pai-lu takes her hand. Unable to control herself, she breaks out into a cry of pain.*)

PAI-LU: What's the matter?

THE SHRIMP (*in pain*): It hurts!

PAI-LU: My God! How could your arm have been so. . . .

THE SHRIMP: It's all right. (*Covering up her arm*) They were afraid I might run away, so they took away my clothes and made me stay in bed.

PAI-LU: What were they doing when you got out?

THE SHRIMP: They were smoking opium and playing mahjong in the next room. Once they were settled I got quietly out of bed and put on some of my mother's clothes.

PAI-LU: Why didn't you run right out?

THE SHRIMP (*practically*): Where would I go? I don't know anybody, and I've got no money.

PAI-LU: What about your mother?

THE SHRIMP: She's upstairs.

PAI-LU: No, I mean your own mother, your real mother.

THE SHRIMP: Oh. (*Her eyes filling with tears*) She's dead, a long time ago.

PAI-LU: And your father?

THE SHRIMP: He died a month ago.

PAI-LU: I see. — But why come in here? They can easily find you.

THE SHRIMP (*terrified*): No, no, no! (*Going down on her knees*) You must help me! You mustn't let them find me, or else they'll kill me! (*Holding on to Pai-lu's hand*) Oh, Miss!

PAI-LU: Get up (*helping her to her feet*), I didn't say I was going to send you back. Now sit down while we think out a way.

THE SHRIMP: All right, then. (*She suddenly slips over to the door and closes it.*)

PAI-LU (*patting her on the shoulder*): Don't worry about that. There's nothing to be afraid of yet.

THE SHRIMP (*trembling*): No, I'm not afraid, I'm not afraid.

PAI-LU: What are you still trembling for, then?

THE SHRIMP (*with bent head*): I'm hungry.

PAI-LU: Why, of course, how stupid of me. (*Going to the food-cupboard*) Haven't you had anything to eat?

THE SHRIMP: No, not for more than a day now. They said they wouldn't let me have anything to eat until the dark fat man was happy.

PAI-LU (*getting her some biscuits*): Here are some biscuits for you to be getting on with.

(*The Shrimp looks at them but does not dare take them.*)

PAI-LU: Come on, have some.

THE SHRIMP (*taking them*): Thank you.

(*The centre door creaks open.*)

THE SHRIMP (*hastily putting down what she is eating and hiding in a corner*): Miss!

PAI-LU: Who is it?

(*Fu-sheng comes in.*)

FU-SHENG: It's me, Miss.

THE SHRIMP (*terrified*): He. . . .

PAI-LU: Don't be frightened, it's only the waiter who looks after me.

FU-SHENG: Miss, the manager of the Ta Feng Bank, Mr. Pan, came here three times last night.

PAI-LU: I know, I know.

FU-SHENG: He's still here.

PAI-LU: Still here? Why doesn't he go?

FU-SHENG: Well, you know there's a big new building going up next door to the hotel? Well, I think Mr. Pan's now talking it over with his secretary. But he said that when you came back I was to go and ask him over.

PAI-LU: If they want to erect a building there's no reason why they shouldn't, but I don't see why they should have to come here in the middle of the night to discuss it.

FU-SHENG: Quite.

PAI-LU: Tell Mr. Pan I'm off to bed now for some sleep.

FU-SHENG: But why won't you see him? After all, Mr. Pan's the manager of a big bank, and —

PAI-LU (*who has had enough of his garrulity*): It's nothing that need concern you. I just don't want to see him.

FU-SHENG (*cringing and smiling obsequiously*): Very good, Miss. (*Taking a sheaf of bills from his pocket*) There are some more bills here, Miss. Do you want me to read them out to you? Mei Feng Jewellers 654 dollars forty, Yung Chang Silk Company 355 dollars fifty-five, the hotel 229 dollars seventy-six, Hung Sheng Studio 117 dollars seventy, Chiu Hua Chang Shoe Shop ninety-one dollars thirty, weekly account for cars seventy-six dollars fifty — oh, and also —

PAI-LU (*finally losing patience*): Stop it, stop reading them out, I can't be bothered to listen.

FU-SHENG: It's not that I don't want to do my best for you, Miss, but I can't keep putting your creditors off like this day after day: whatever you say about it, if you haven't got cash again today I'll just have to give up.

PAI-LU (*with a sigh*): Money, money, always money! (*With annoyance*) I wish you wouldn't keep bothering me with these things!

FU-SHENG: It's not my fault, Miss, but things are tight this year and credit's difficult to get. You don't know today whether tomorrow —

PAI-LU: I've never yet asked anyone to help me out with money.

FU-SHENG: There's no doubt about your good standing, Miss; all the same —

PAI-LU: All right, I'll soon find some way of settling up, you can set their minds at rest about that.

FU-SHENG: All right. (*Just as he is about to leave*) Why, Miss, what's this little girl doing here?
(*The Shrimp looks imploringly at Pai-lu.*)

PAI-LU (*going over to the Shrimp*): Nothing that need concern you.

FU-SHENG (*looking the Shrimp up and down*): I seem to recognize her. Now Miss, you mustn't go looking for trouble.

PAI-LU: What do you mean?

FU-SHENG: There's somebody searching for her outside.

PAI-LU: Who?

FU-SHENG: A gang of toughs from upstairs, strong-arm men every one of them.

THE SHRIMP (*crying out in fear*): Oh, Miss. (*Going across to Fu-sheng and imploring him*) Oh, Uncle!

FU-SHENG: Keep away from me!

PAI-LU (*to Fu-sheng*): Shut the door! And lock it.

FU-SHENG: But Miss —

PAI-LU: Lock the door.

FU-SHENG (*locking the door*): You'll never hide her, Miss. Her mother and father are ransacking the building for her.

PAI-LU: If we give them some money they'll be satisfied, surely?

FU-SHENG: You're getting generous again. Give them some money? How many thousands have you got?

PAI-LU: How do you mean?

FU-SHENG: Give them some now and they'll soak you for every penny you've got.

PAI-LU: Then we'd —

(*Sound of footsteps and voices outside.*)

FU-SHENG: Quiet! There's someone outside. (*Listening a moment*) It's them, they're here.

THE SHRIMP (*unable to restrain herself*): Oh, what can we do?

PAI-LU (*gripping her hand tightly*): If you make one more sound, I'll bundle you outside.

THE SHRIMP (*in a hushed voice*): No, no!

PAI-LU (*in a low voice*): Be quiet, then.

BLACK SAN'S VOICE (*explosively*): The little bitch, she's more trouble than she's worth, throwing away the chance of a lifetime and running away like this. I'm damned if I know what fathered her.

WOMAN'S VOICE: I ask you, here's somebody rolling in money comes along and all this heartless child can do is to bolt. That's going to take some explaining away, I can tell you.

BLACK SAN'S VOICE (*bellowing impatiently at the woman*): You bloody well clear out of it. The kid's bolted, through you not keeping an eye on her, and all you can do is keep on clack-clack-clacking.

(*No further sound from the woman.*)

BLACK SAN: Here, you don't think she could have got outside, do you?

SECOND MAN'S VOICE: No, no chance of that.

WOMAN'S VOICE: She ran off in my coat. She couldn't get far like that. Yet nobody's seen her, they say, on the ground floor or the first.

THIRD MAN'S VOICE: That waiter on this floor said he'd just seen her.

BLACK SAN'S VOICE (*harshly authoritative*): Then she *must* be on this floor so let's get on with it and find her.

WOMAN'S VOICE (*snarling*): She won't escape, anyway, the little bitch.

(*The three people in the room listen with straining ears and bated breath as the footsteps of the men and the woman die away.*)

PAI-LU: They've gone.

FU-SHENG: Yes, probably round to the other side.

PAI-LU (*suddenly opening the door*): Let me have a look. (*Just as she is going to put her head out, the Shrimp seizes her by the hand and pulls her back in desperation.*)

FU-SHENG (*shutting the door, warningly*): You don't want to get mixed up with them.

PAI-LU (*to the Shrimp*): Don't be afraid, it's all right. (*To Fu-sheng*) Now what do you mean —

FU-SHENG: Don't get on the wrong side of them. People like that can be nasty if you annoy them. Only a fool goes looking for trouble.

PAI-LU: What do you mean?

FU-SHENG: They don't go about empty-handed, any of them. They get their living by risking their necks.

PAI-LU: But surely they must have some respect for law! After treating a child like this, look (*holding up the Shrimp's arm*), stabbed her with opium-needles. If they insist on making a nuisance of themselves I'll sue them.

FU-SHENG (*scornfully*): Sue them? You'd have a hope? They're in with all the people who matter here, so how can you sue them? Even if you won your case,

what chance would you have when they came to even
the score?

PAI-LU: Surely you don't expect me to hand the child
over to them?

THE SHRIMP (*hoarse with terror*): No, don't, Miss. (*She
wipes the tears that have begun to trickle with her
outsize sleeve.*)

FU-SHENG (*shaking his head*): It's an awkward business. I think you'd better do the sensible thing and
take the child back to them. I hear she slapped Mr.
Chin's face and upset him. Didn't you realize that?

PAI-LU (*taken aback*): What, him? (*Looking at the
Shrimp, worried*) Child, child!

FU-SHENG: Just think: Mr. Chin, the God of Wealth
himself, a man of money and influence, and this gang
of toughs are in his pay. My God!

PAI-LU: So that's who it was. What would he be doing
here, in this hotel?

FU-SHENG: If he gets fed up with staying at home and
chooses to come here for a night out, why shouldn't
he? After all, he's rolling in money.

PAI-LU (*to herself*): Chin. (*To the Shrimp*) To think
you had to fall foul of a monster like that. — *Did*
you slap his face, Shrimp?

THE SHRIMP: You mean the dark fat man? — Yes.
He — he wanted to — I couldn't get away and somehow
I hit him.

PAI-LU (*to herself*): Well done! Well done! I hope
it hurt him!

FU-SHENG (*afraid of trouble*): Miss, I must make it
quite clear that I'm not in on this business. If you
want to play the good Samaritan and take this girl
under your wing, then you do it on your own, it's got
nothing to do with me. If they ask me about it
presently —

PAI-LU (*bluntly*): Then you haven't seen her!

FU-SHENG (*looking at the Shrimp, uneasily*): Haven't seen her? But —

PAI-LU: If anything goes wrong I shall answer for it.

FU-SHENG (*who was hoping that she would say just this*): All right, all right, you answer for it, then. (*Glibly*) Witness the electric light above and the floor beneath that you yourself said it.

PAI-LU (*nodding*): Yes, of course, when I say a thing I mean it. Now ask Mr. Pan to come in.

FU-SHENG: But didn't you say just now that you didn't want him in?

PAI-LU: Do as I tell you and don't stand there drivelling —

FU-SHENG (*in a drawling voice*): Very well — very well — very well — (*He goes out in a huff.*)

PAI-LU (*to the Shrimp*): Had enough to eat?

THE SHRIMP (*dazedly*): Yes.

PAI-LU (*looking at the biscuits in her hand*): But you haven't eaten any yet!

THE SHRIMP: I can't, I'm afraid, I'm terrified — (*She bursts out crying.*)

PAI-LU (*coming across to comfort her*): Don't cry! Don't cry!

THE SHRIMP: Miss, you won't take me back to them, will you?

PAI-LU: No, I won't. Now stop crying, stop crying. Listen, someone outside!

(*The Shrimp at once stops.*)

(*Mr. Pan, the bank manager, comes in. He is a massive creature swathed in silk with greying hair and ponderous movements, but when he sees Pai-lu his years fall from him and in his actions and manner he suddenly becomes young and lively, though in fact his youngest son is past twenty. His eyes are narrow slits and his nose like a Pekinese dog's; he has a thin drooping moustache, a large mouth, and a gold tooth that gleams ostentatiously when his lips part in a jocular*) *smile. He is wearing a dark brown gown lined with otter-fur with a sleeveless satin jacket over it, hung with a gold watch-chain and an emerald pendant. He seems to have just dressed, for his collar-button has not yet been done up. He has a cigar in one hand and although his brows are creased into a frown he cannot keep a smile from his lips.)*

PAN: Pai-lu, I knew you'd send for me! I've been waiting all night for you. Fortunately, Li Shih-ching turned up to see me about some bank business. Otherwise I wouldn't have known how to kill time. I sent someone up to you several times, but you hadn't got back. Well, now, I ask you to dine with me and you won't; I ask you to go dancing with me and you won't go; but *(with great satisfaction)* I knew you'd send for me sooner or later.

PAI-LU *(sliding him a look out of the corner of her eye)*: You're very sure of your powers of fascination, aren't you?

PAN *(self-confidently)*: Pity you couldn't have seen me when I was young. *(In a low voice)* I knew you were thinking of me *(trying to sound sentimental)*, weren't you?

PAI-LU: Yes, I was thinking of you —

PAN: There you are, I knew it. *(Gesturing towards her)* Your heart's in the right place.

PAI-LU: Yes, I was thinking of you and me tackling a job together.

PAN *(putting on a frown)*: Tackling a job again. — Is that all you can think of when you see me? No time for anything but getting mixed up in things that don't concern you.

PAI-LU: How do you know?

PAN: Fu-sheng told me all about it.

PAI-LU: Are you on?

PAN *(going across to the Shrimp)*: Well, so this is the little shrimp.

PAI-LU: Look at the poor little thing, she —

PAN: All right, all right, I know all about it. That's what always happens, anyway.

PAI-LU (*menacingly*): Well, Yueh-ting, are you on?

PAN: Yes, I'm on!

PAI-LU: Well, Shrimp, aren't you going to thank Mr. Pan?

(*The Shrimp is about to go up to him.*)

PAN (*stopping her*): No, no, don't start that. Pai-lu, you're a great burden to me.

PAI-LU: Listen!

(*Voices outside.*)

PAI-LU: It sounds as if they're back again. Shrimp, you go in that room. (*She indicates the door on the right.*)

(*The Shrimp goes into the next room.*)

BLACK SAN'S VOICE (*from outside*): This door?

SECOND MAN'S VOICE: That's the one.

PAI-LU (*to Pan*): They probably mean my door.

PAN: Yes.

BLACK SAN'S VOICE: You're sure it was this door you saw her go in?

SECOND MAN'S VOICE: Yes.

BLACK SAN'S VOICE: And she didn't come out?

WOMAN'S VOICE: What's the matter with you? You find the door and then stand there dithering about.

THIRD MAN'S VOICE: No, we've got to be sure, we mustn't go in the wrong one.

(*Muffled confused sound of men's voices.*)

PAI-LU: You mustn't wait for them to come in, Yueh-ting. Open the door and go out and tell them to clear off.

PAN: They probably know me, these fellows, so I shouldn't have much trouble getting rid of them.

PAI-LU: That's good, Yueh-ting, thank you, thank you, you're one of the best.

PAN (*smiling naively*): That's the first time since I've known you that you've thanked me for anything.

PAI-LU (*teasing him*): That's because it's the first time you've been one of the best.

PAN: There you go again, Pai-lu, making fun of me, you —

PAI-LU: Now stop talking and go and send them away.

PAN: Very well. (*Just as he is about to go out* —)

PAI-LU: You do realize, of course, Yueh-ting, that it was Mr. Chin who took a fancy to the girl.

PAN: Mr. Chin? (*He takes his hand from the doorhandle.*)

PAI-LU: She offended Mr. Chin.

PAN: Oh, so she's a girl that Mr. Chin's taken a fancy to, is she?

PAI-LU: Didn't Fu-sheng tell you?

PAN: No, he didn't; whew, you nearly had the fat in the fire.

(*He shrinks back.*)

PAI-LU: You mean to say you've changed your mind, Yueh-ting?

PAN: Don't you realize, Pai-lu, that this fellow Chin has all kinds of dubious connections and that he's no great respecter of persons?

PAI-LU: You're calling it off, then?

PAN: It's not that I won't do it: I can't. Anyway, for the sake of a mere country girl like this, why do you have to go and —

PAI-LU (*offended*): Very well, then. If you won't do it that's that, but there's no need for you to try and stop me doing it.

PAN: There, there, no need to be like that about it.

THIRD MAN'S VOICE OUTSIDE (*roughly*): Knock on the door, she's in there right enough.

BLACK SAN'S VOICE: Why?

THIRD MAN'S VOICE: Look, Ma's handkerchief, isn't it? Well, the girl was wearing Ma's coat when she escaped, wasn't she?

WOMAN'S VOICE: Yes, that's right, that is my handkerchief.

BLACK SAN'S VOICE: Then it must be this door, this must be where she is. Open up there! Open up!

PAI-LU (*teasing Pan*): Now don't be afraid, Yueh-ting! (*She goes to open the door to them.*)

PAN (*grasping Pai-lu's hand*): Take no notice of them.

VOICES OUTSIDE: Open up there!

PAI-LU: Yueh-ting, you go in that room so that it won't be awkward for you. I shall open the door.

PAN: No, Pai-lu, don't.

PAI-LU: Go on in. (*Pointing to the door on the left*) Go on in — I'll be really cross with you.

PAN: All right, I'll go.

PAI-LU: Hurry!
(*Pan goes into the room on the left and Pai-lu immediately opens the centre door wide.*)

PAI-LU (*to those outside*): What do you want here?
(*Black San is standing outside the door in black clothes and a felt hat.*)

BLACK SAN: What do we want? (*Boisterously, to his colleagues outside*) Come on in, all of you, search the place.

PAI-LU (*a sudden sense of outrage showing in her voice and expression*): Stop! All come in? Who said anything about all of you coming in? Who do you think you are, anyway? If you try any rough stuff here, while the boss of the manor's here, you'll find he can be just as rough! (*Smiling*) Is it contraband you're looking for? If it's opium you're looking for you'll find plenty here, and guns too, if that's what you're after (*squaring her shoulders*), and I'm not kidding you, either! (*Pointing to the room on the left*) In there I've got five hundred taels of opium (*pointing to the room on the right)*, and in there I've got eighty revolvers, so tell me, what do you want? That little lot should be enough for all of you to amuse yourselves with. (*The men in the doorway have been brought to a halt by this outburst, and she continues speaking through the doorway.*) Do come in, gentlemen! (*With a great show of politeness*) Why don't you come in? Why, what's the matter? What are you afraid of?

THIRD MAN (*in his bovine manner*): In we go, then, if we're going! What's stopping us?

BLACK SAN: Get out, you idiot, who told you to come in?

THIRD MAN (*dully*): Out, then, if that's what you want. It's all the same to me.

BLACK SAN (*smiling*): Now don't — don't upset yourself. No need to fly off the handle at people. Don't think we'd come and disturb you without a very good reason. We've had a little girl run away from us, a little first time girl she is, and what we came here for was to look for her, in case she was hiding somewhere and might frighten you later on.

PAI-LU: Oh, I see. (*As if she suddenly understands*) So all you people are here looking for a little girl!

BLACK SAN (*with sharpening interest*): Then I expect you must have seen her come in.

PAI-LU: I'm sorry, I haven't.

BLACK SAN: But look, we found a handkerchief that she'd dropped outside your door.

PAI-LU: Well, if she will go and drop it what can I do about it?

BLACK SAN: Ah, but let me tell you something else: somebody saw her come in here a short while ago.

PAI-LU: If she's been in my suite I'll tell you this now: if she's stolen anything of mine you'll have to pay for it.

BLACK SAN: Cut out the funny stuff, please. As likely as not we're in the same racket, so you might give us a helping hand. I can see that Mr. Chin means the same to you as to us —

PAI-LU: Mr. Chin? Oh, are you friends of Mr. Chin, too?

BLACK SAN (*smiling*): Not up to being his friends, quite, we just do odd little jobs for him.

PAI-LU: Well, that's all right, then. Mr. Chin was just this moment telling me to tell you to clear off.

BLACK SAN: Just this moment, you say?

PAI-LU (*who has no alternative but to go through with it now that she has gone this far*): Mr. Chin's in here, as it happens.

BLACK SAN (*dubious*): In here? But we saw Mr. Chin off from the hotel just now.

PAI-LU: But you didn't know that he'd come back.

BLACK SAN: Come back? (*Pausing and sensing the lie*) Then we'd better see him and tell him how we're getting on. (*Turning and speaking through the doorway*) Hadn't we?

VOICES FROM THE DOORWAY: Yes, yes, we ought to see him.

PAI-LU (*calmly*): I'm sorry, but Mr. Chin is not at home to visitors.

BLACK SAN: He can't refuse to see me. I must see him.

PAI-LU: Well, you can't.

BLACK SAN: It's not a matter of can't, it's a matter of must. (*Seeing Pai-lu go towards the room on the right where the Shrimp is hiding*) Mr. Chin's probably in this room.

PAI-LU (*suddenly dashing across to the door of the room on the left where Pan is hiding and standing in front of it*): Yes, you go in that room.

BLACK SAN: Aha — so Mrs. Chin is up to her funny stuff again, is she? (*Smiling mirthlessly at Pai-lu as he comes across to her, then, fiercely*) Out of it! Out of my way!

PAI-LU: You'll get your head bitten off, I expect. (*Turning and speaking through the door*) Mr. Chin, Mr. Chin, come out and tell this gang of idiots where they get off. (*The door opens and Pan Yueh-ting emerges in a dressing gown.*)

PAN (*pointing inside the room and speaking in a low voice*): What's all this noise, Pai-lu? Mr. Chin's asleep. (*Looking at the man*) Why, it's you, Black San! What are you up to?

BLACK SAN: Oh (*taken aback*), so you're here, too, Mr. Pan.

PAN: I come in here with Mr. Chin to rest my legs for a moment and have a smoke, and here are you, coming in here to have a rebellion.   What's it all about?

BLACK SAN (*faltering*):   Oh, Mr. Chin is here after all. (*Laughing nervously*) Uhuh, he's having a sleep here, is he?

PAN: Did you want to come in and have a chat with him? Please come in and sit down, then! (*Throwing the door wide open*) I'll roast you a bead of opium and get Mr. Chin up to entertain you, shall I?

BLACK SAN (*smiling obsequiously*):   Don't make fun of us like this, Mr. Pan.

PAN: You won't sit down? Won't those gentlemen in the doorway there come in for a rest?

BLACK SAN: No, no, we're still busy with a job, you see —

PAN: Excellent. If you're busy, then please be so good as to scram instead of standing there talking nonsense!

BLACK SAN (*obediently*): Very well, Mr. Pan, but please don't get so angry.   I hope you'll forgive us if we've offended you.   (*Suddenly turning his head and addressing those in the doorway*) What are you all staring at? Go on, get out of it, you rabble! Bloody thick-headed lot! (*Turning back with a smile*) You see? What can you do with a crowd like that? Mr. Pan, when Mr. Chin wakes up later on please don't on any account let him

know that we've been here. And you must put in a
good word for us, Miss. And please don't breathe a
word about what happened just now. Look on it as a
joke on my part, what happened just now. I don't
deserve to live. (*Striking himself across the mouth*) I
deserve to be hanged for it.

PAI-LU: All right, now hurry up and get out.

BLACK SAN (*obsequiously*): I hope you're not angry
with us any longer? It's all right, we're going now. (*He
goes out.*)

PAI-LU (*closing the door*): That's that, then. (*To herself*)
It's the first time I've done anything so satisfying.

PAN: That's that, as you say. It's the first time I've
done anything so absurd.

PAI-LU: Well, now you can go and ask the almighty Mr.
Chin to resume his throne.

PAN: Humph! "It's easier to raise the Devil than to send
him away." It's easy enough to get rid of them with a
piece of bluff like that, but the next time we run into
Mr. Chin there's going to be hell to pay, as likely as
not.

PAI-LU: We won't worry about tomorrow until it
comes. Anyway, it was great fun.

PAN: Fun?

PAI-LU: I think anything can be fun. Don't you agree?
(*Yawning*) I *am* tired. (*Suddenly catching sight of the
sunlight on the floor*) I say, look! Look at that!

PAN: Eh? What?

PAI-LU: The sun, the *sun's* up. (*She hurries across to
the window.*)

PAN (*drily*): Well, there's nothing wrong with the sun
getting up if it wants to. Why all the shouting about
it?

PAI-LU (*looking out of the sun-filled window, through
which comes the faint chirping of sparrows*): Look how
blue the sky is! (*The chirping of sparrows can be heard
outside the window.*) There, listen, sparrows! Spring's

here. (*With great feeling, her heart filled with happiness*) Oh! I love the sun, I love the spring, I love being young, I love being me. Oh! I'm on top of the world! (*She draws a deep breath of the chill air.*)

PAN (*uninterested*): Well, there's no harm in feeling like that, though I don't see what all the fuss is about. (*Suddenly*) Pai-lu, it's too cold in here. You'll be frozen. I'll shut the window for you.

PAI-LU (*obstinately*): No, I don't want it shut! I don't want it shut!

PAN: All right, all right, leave it open if you want to. You're a great trial to me, child; even my own daughter I never took so much trouble over as I do over you.

PAI-LU (*looking round*): What's so unusual about that? Would you still be taking so much trouble over me if I were your daughter?

PAN: I asked for that, a very penetrating remark. (*Seriously*) Come on, then, shut the window or I'll be catching . . . catching . . . (*mouth open and eyes wrinkled as if about to sneeze*) catching . . . (*a violent sneeze*) there, I've already caught a cold.

PAI-LU (*suddenly coming back from the window*): You silly boy, why didn't you say so before?

PAN (*with satisfaction*): Now perhaps you'll shut the window.

PAI-LU (*shaking her head*): No, I won't do that, I'll give you something more to put on. Come along now, sit down, with my overcoat round your shoulders, and my scarf round your neck, and your fur-lined gown over you, and you can have this hot-water bottle of mine, too. There, that's better, isn't it? (*Arranging the old man in a bizarre-looking heap on the sofa*) I'm very fond of you really, you're just like a father to me. My poor Daddy, we do treat you badly here, don't we!

PAN (*pushing her away*): Pai-lu (*trying to get up*), I won't have you calling me Daddy.

PAI-LU (*pushing him till he topples back on to the sofa again*): If I want to call you Daddy then I'll call you Daddy. My old Daddy.

PAN (*protesting*): I'm not old, why should you call me an old daddy?

PAI-LU (*petulantly*): I'm going to call you it, so there! My old Daddy! My old Daddy!

PAN (*in a better humour now*): Call me it, I don't mind! I like it, I like it. (*He beams with delight.*)

PAI-LU (*suddenly*): Now sit still, Yueh-ting, and I'll read you a story. (*She picks up a handsomely bound book.*)

PAN: I don't want to listen to a story.

PAI-LU: You must.

PAN: Oh, all right, I'll listen. (*Catching sight of the title of the book*) Sunrise, no, that's no good, title's no good to start with.

PAI-LU: Yes, it is! Because *I* say it is.

PAN: All right, all right, you read, then.

PAI-LU (*finding a place in the book and reading aloud*): ". . . The sun is risen, and the darkness is left behind."

PAN (*yawning and stretching*): Doesn't make sense, no sense at all in it.

PAI-LU (*ignoring him and reading on*): " . . . But the sun is not for us, for we shall be asleep."

PAN (*yawning deeply*): That doesn't make sense either, though there's something in that last bit: "We shall be asleep."

PAI-LU (*closing the book impatiently*): Oh, you're impossible. You're not to keep interrupting. If you say another word I'll — (*She raises the book to hit him.*) (*From the bedroom on the right comes the yapping of a Pekinese dog mingled with cries of alarm from the Shrimp.*)

PAN: What's that?

(*Pai-lu gets up.*)

(The Shrimp runs out of the bedroom. She closes the door in alarm, leaving the dog barking under it from inside.)

THE SHRIMP *(panic-stricken)*:   Miss, Miss!

PAI-LU: What's the matter?

THE SHRIMP: He . . . he's after me.

PAI-LU *(in consternation)*: What! Who? Who?

THE SHRIMP *(breathless with fright)*: Your dog's woken up. *(Looking behind her)* He was trying to bite me.

PAI-LU: You silly child! I thought for a moment that those people were coming in through the bedroom!

PAN: There, see what you're in for?

(A knock on the door.)

THE SHRIMP *(looking at Pai-lu)*:   There's somebody at the door.

PAN: Not them back again, I hope?

PAI-LU *(going to the door)*:   Who is it?

(The door opens and Fang Ta-sheng comes in.)

TA-SHENG: It's me, Chu-chun.

PAI-LU *(taken aback)*: Why aren't you in bed?

TA-SHENG: I can't get to sleep in this place, it's too noisy. The waiter's been telling me you've just acquired an adopted daughter.

PAI-LU: An adopted daughter?

TA-SHENG: Yes.

PAI-LU: Oh, I see what you mean. *(Indicating the Shrimp)* This is her. My adopted daughter. We call her the Shrimp.

TA-SHENG *(interested)*: The Shrimp, eh?

PAN *(rising from his heap of clothes in a brightly-coloured scarf and an overcoat which almost completely envelops him)*: Now, now, Pai-lu, don't stand there chatting away like that. Who is this gentleman?

PAI-LU: Don't you know? Let me introduce you. This is my cousin.

PAN *(surprised)*:   Your cousin?

TA-SHENG (*realizing for the first time that there is another man in the room, to Pai-lu*): What's this? Who's he?

PAI-LU (*keeping a perfectly straight face*): Why, don't you know who this is? My Daddy.

TA-SHENG (*taken aback*): Your Daddy?

PAN (*to Pai-lu, jokingly*): Well, all one happy family! (*Suddenly, pointing to the window*) But do hurry up and shut . . . shut . . . (*still gesturing towards the window*) . . . shut . . . (*He sneezes.*) There, I really have caught a cold this time.

—*QUICK CURTAIN*—

Act II

The scene is as in Act One, still the luxuriously-furnished sitting-room of a suite in the X hotel.

It is getting dark and the room is filled with the light of the setting sun. From outside the window comes the rhythmical sound of pile-driving songs from the labourers laying the foundations of the new building next to the hotel. The sound gradually moves farther away and is mingled with the tramp of many feet and the heavy thump of the stone rammers against the ground. The labourers here sing two different pile-driving songs: the Hsiao Hai Hao and the Chou Hao. At the moment they are engaged on the Hsiao Hai Hao, with one shrill voice singing the lead-line and twenty or thirty voices answering in chorus. Sandwiched between the two, as the voices pause for a moment, comes the earth-ramming chant of two or three teams of men with "rammers."

When the curtain rises Fu-sheng is alone in the room tidying up the ash-trays, cigarette-boxes and so forth, an expression of great impatience on his face; he is continually glancing out of the window and yawning.

FU-SHENG (*unable to bear it any longer, he turns to the window and spits with contempt*): Bah! "Hai-ai!" Nothing but bloody "hai-ai!" They'll have driven us all mad by the time this building's finished.

(*Now comes the distant sound of the labourers swinging their stone rammers against the ground and singing the Hsiao Hai Hao.*)

FU-SHENG (*after listening for a moment, viciously*): Still at it! When it's as much as I can do to snatch forty

43

winks in the daytime, this lot of so-and-so's have to
keep on bawling all the time without a stop! Now that
it's nearly dark you'd think they'd get fed up with it:
like hell they do! (*He spits again.*)
(*The chanting becomes louder and louder, and now they
change the tune and begin singing the* Chu Hao:
   "*The sun comes up from the East,*
   The sky is a great red glow.
   If we want rice to eat
   We must bend our backs in toil.")

FU-SHENG (*he suddenly sits down and takes out the two
 balls of paper that he has stuffed into his ears; he rubs
 round the inside of his ears with his fingers. Challengingly*): Come on, then! Sing up! Let's hear your hai-ai-
 ing! Now that I'm stuck with you! I'll listen and you
 sing, and we'll bloody soon see who gives in first! (*Closing his eyes determinedly*) See who gives in first!
 (*The singing begins to fade and Fang Ta-sheng comes
 in.*)

FU-SHENG (*rising and looking round when he becomes
 aware that there is someone behind him*): Oh, it's Mr.
 Fang. Up already?

TA-SHENG (*not understanding why he says this*): Why,
 of course — it'll soon be dark.

FU-SHENG (*glad to have an audience to air his grievances
 to*): I don't wonder you're up! No chance of sleeping
 with this rabble out here. Need their necks wringing —

TA-SHENG (*gesturing towards the window*): Shh! Listen!

FU-SHENG: What to?

TA-SHENG (*pointing towards the window, his interest
 fully aroused*): Listen, listen to them singing, don't
 talk.

FU-SHENG (*taken aback*): Oh, singing you call it.

TA-SHENG (*curtly*): Yes.
 (*Outside they are singing:*
   "*The sun sinks in the West,*
   We ram till our patience is gone.

> We must barter our lives away
> Or none will show us pity."

As the last line ends, for some reason there is a roar of laughter, but immediately the steady, rhythmical heng-heng-yo, heng-heng-yo of the labourers is heard again as they advance pounding the earth with their rammers.)

TA-SHENG (*leaning against the window and looking down delightedly*): What wonderful singing!

FU-SHENG (*surprised*): Wonderful, you say?

TA-SHENG (*sighing, but happily*): Just look at them, their faces streaming with sweat, singing away.

FU-SHENG (*with a sardonic smile*): Born to slave in poverty. If they weren't, you don't think they'd be spending their lives pile-driving, just mere labourers, putting up buildings for other people to live in!

TA-SHENG: Who's building this place?

FU-SHENG: Whoever it is you can be sure they've got plenty of money.   It's being built by the Ta Feng Bank, by Mr. Pan, and I shouldn't be surprised if (*pointing to the room on the left*) Mrs. Ku in there hasn't got a hand in it, too. *Dispiritedly)* And what do they do with their money! (*Gesturing at random*) Put up big buildings like that with it. (*Feeling sorry for himself*) The more money they have, the more they make!

TA-SHENG: Mrs. Ku? You mean that old hag with her face plastered in paint and powder?

FU-SHENG: Yes, that's her! Mutton dressed up like lamb, doesn't realize how old she is; but she's rich, so of course everybody tells her how young and beautiful she is.   Even Mr. Pan praises her up, to say nothing of all the others.   You saw Mr. Pan go in there (*pointing to the room on the left*) with Miss Chen and Mrs. Ku to play mahjong, didn't you? I tell you, she's rolling in it.

TA-SHENG: But I've been out quite a while since that. You mean that these (*distastefully*) people are still in there playing mahjong? Not gone yet?

FU-SHENG: Gone? Where to? It'll be dark soon and there'll be a lot more people coming, and then they'll be even less likely to go.

TA-SHENG (*pacing up and down the room a couple of times*): This place is really depressing. It's horrible, horrible.

(*There is a knock on the door.*)

TA-SHENG: Who is it? (*No reply.*) Another of them.

FU-SHENG: Who is it? (*He goes to open the door.*)

TA-SHENG (*stopping him*): Wait a minute while I go in here. (*He goes through the door on the right into Pai-lu's bedroom.*)

FU-SHENG (*distastefully*): My, my, we *are* particular, aren't we! (*He opens the centre door.*)

(*Huang Hsing-san comes timidly in. His pallid face is quite devoid of any colour and his expression is one of great embarrassment and fearfulness. His limbs are as thin as sticks and he is wearing only a pair of lined trousers and an old, faded, thin wadded gown. He is a timid man and also extremely nervous and he wears the same bleak and cheerless look even when he smiles. It costs him a great deal of effort to speak each sentence—and even then his voice is low—and when he has finally got it out he coughs a couple of times, unable to help himself. He is so humble and lacking in self-confidence that he is afraid that even the sound of his voice may make one lose patience with him. He is not particularly old, but years of worry and overwork have made him almost into an old man.*)

(*He stands timidly in the doorway looking all round.*)

FU-SHENG: So it's you here again! (*His face taking on a hard look*) What are you doing here?

HUANG (*his voice shaking*): I'm sorry! (*With an apologetic laugh*) I — I'm sorry! (*Bowing*) I — I must have come to the wrong door. (*He coughs and turns to go out.*)

FU-SHENG (*hauling him back*): Come here! Come back! Where do you think you're going?

HUANG (*his face flushing as he hastens to excuse himself*): I came to the wrong door, sir.

FU-SHENG: Wrong door or not, back you must come. This doesn't happen to be one of the doors that you are entitled to barge in through just as you like.

HUANG: But sir, I made a mistake, and I've — I've apologized.

FU-SHENG: Don't you realize there are all kinds of people in the hotel? Why didn't you knock instead of just barging straight in?

HUANG (*with a nervous smile*): I — I did knock, sir —

FU-SHENG (*prevaricating*): Then how is it I didn't hear you?

HUANG (*smiling miserably*): How can I help it, sir, if you didn't hear me? (*Pitifully*) Let me go now, sir. (*He turns away.*)

FU-SHENG: Dolt! Who do you want, anyway?

HUANG (*fumbling uneasily with his scarf*): I've — I've come to see Mr. Li.

FU-SHENG: There are dozens of Li's; which one's "Mr." Li?

HUANG: No (*hastening to explain*), no, I mean I was looking for number fifty-two.

FU-SHENG: This is room number fifty-two.

HUANG (*unable to conceal his delight*): Then, then I was right all the time. (*Turning to Fu-sheng again, politely*) I'd like to see Mr. Li Shih-ching.

FU-SHENG: He's not here.

HUANG (*after hesitating a long time*): If Mr. Pan the bank-manager isn't busy I'd like to see him instead. Would you mind telling him, sir?

FU-SHENG (*sizing him up*): Well, there *is* a Mr. Pan, but (*acidly*) you? You'd like to see Mr. Pan?

HUANG (*desperately*): I'm — a clerk at the Ta Feng Bank.

FU-SHENG: A clerk? In that case even the mention of your illustrious ancestors won't cut any ice with a man like Mr. Pan. He only drops in for a social call and he's never at home to visitors here.

HUANG: But (*imploringly*), sir, you *will* just go and ask him if he'll see me, won't you?

FU-SHENG: He's not here! (*Losing patience*) I tell you Mr. Pan's not here! Now be off out of it and don't keep making a nuisance of yourself. You come here a complete stranger, butting in here trying to see people, there's no telling what you mayn't be up to!

HUANG (*in another attempt to explain*): But sir, I—I'm a clerk at the Ta Feng Bank, and my name's Huang—

FU-SHENG (*suddenly turning squarely to Huang and pointing to himself*): Do you know me?

HUANG (*after looking at him for a while*): No, I can't say I do.

FU-SHENG: Then quick march! (*Pushing him*) Go on, out!

HUANG: But sir, my name's Huang. . . .

FU-SHENG (*opening the door and pushing him outside*): Go on, out! Out! Stop making such a nuisance of yourself. If you come here again I'll—

HUANG (*over his shoulder as he is pushed out*): Sir, my name's Huang, Huang Hsing-san, I used to be—

FU-SHENG (*haughtily*): I know, you used to be a clerk, your name's Huang Hsing-san, you want to see Mr. Li, you want to see Mr. Pan, in fact you want to see everybody from the Ta Feng Bank. You're going round everywhere pretending to be something you're not and trying to get a job. You think I don't know all about it? Think I don't know you?

HUANG (*his hands shaking on account of his overwrought feelings*): If you know me, sir (*smiling submissively*), that's better still.

FU-SHENG (*happily abusing him*): I've seen you here at the hotel time and again but you don't recognize me at all.   You imagine you're going to find a job with a memory like that, you cuckold? (*Seizing hold of Huang and giving him no chance to explain as he thrusts him forcibly outside*) Now clear off out of it, damn you!

HUANG (*staggering and falling over, almost paralysed*): Why should you call me names? I know I'm poor, but you can't call me that, you, you can't —

FU-SHENG (*maliciously*):   You'd better ask your wife about that, how should I know? (*Clapping him on the shoulder and grinning sardonically*) All right, then, you're not a cuckold, your son's a cuckold's brat, how's that?

HUANG (*he suddenly stands up furiously and raises his hand as if he intends to hurl the entire weight of his body on this creature before him and crush him to death*):   You — you — I'll. . . .

FU-SHENG (*every inch the ruffian, he shoots up his eyebrows and seizes Huang by the front of his gown*): You'll do what?   If you so much as lift a finger I'll kill you!
(*A pause.*)

HUANG (*his eyes, glaring like the eyes of a madman, stare at Fu-sheng with a mixture of fear and anger and his hands tremble uncontrollably.   After a while he speaks in a low, feeble voice*): Let — me — go!   Let — me—go!
(*Fu-sheng releases him and he goes out with bent head. Outside, the sad, melancholy heng-heng-yo-heng-heng-yo of the labourers is heard again.*)
(*The telephone rings. Fu-sheng goes to the small table and picks up the receiver.*)

FU-SHENG: Hullo, who is it? (*Unable to hear clearly, raising his voice*) I said who is it? Who do you want? (*Explosively*) Tell me who you want! . . .   Swear at me, will you? . . . And the same to you! . . . What? (*His voice dropping*) Your name's Chin? Oh . . . So. . . . Oh, I see, sir, it's Mr. Chin! . . . Yes. . . . Yes. . . . Yes. . . .

This is room number 52. . . . I couldn't see who it was, I didn't know it was you, sir. . . . (*With an obsequious smile*) Call me what you like, sir! (*He stands to attention bobbing and bowing repeatedly though quite unconsciously, listening with a beaming face to the stream of vile abuse that is being poured into his ear.*) Yes. . . . Yes. . . . I deserve every word of it! It's just as you say, sir!

(*Pan Yueh-ting comes in through the door on the left.*)

PAN (*to Fu-sheng*): Who is it? Who's ringing? Is it Mr. Li Shih-ching?

FU-SHENG (*in a quandary, uncertain which of them he should give his attention to, and shaking his head at Pan Yueh-ting*): . . . No, I wouldn't dare. . . . No, I won't dare do it again. . . . Yes. . . . Now please don't get angry, sir. . . . (*It would appear that his interlocutor's anger is now somewhat abated.*) Yes, I am a bastard . . . yes, you wanted Mr. Pan? Just a moment, sir, he's coming right away. (*To Pan*) For you, sir. (*He is just going to hand over the receiver when the voice begins again. He hastily replaces it at his ear.*) Yes, yes, I'm not of human parentage. (*Handing over the receiver*) I'm an idiot. (*He heaves a long sigh.*)

PAN (*his hand over the mouthpiece, in a low voice*): You stupid idiot! Who is it?

FU-SHENG (*in such a state that he cannot think clearly*): Eh? Who is it? . . . Oh, er, it's Mr. Chin, Mr. Chin.

PAN (*to Fu-sheng*): Has Mr. Li Shih-ching come yet?

FU-SHENG: No, not yet. Mr. Li hasn't come yet.

PAN: Go in and ask Mrs. Li what time her husband said he'd be here.

FU-SHENG: Very good, sir. (*He goes dispiritedly out.*)

PAN (*clearing his throat*): Is that Mr. Chin? . . . This is Yueh-ting. . . . Yes . . . yes, there won't be any trouble about your deposit. If you'll just hold on for three days, and then come for it, I can definitely let you have it. . . . Yes . . . yes . . . the Ta Feng Bank's doing good business at the moment, and I've made a bit on my government bonds — Salt-tax and Disbandment, so don't — eh?... That's right, made a bit on both. So don't worry, three days, and your deposit in the Ta Feng will definitely be repaid in full.... What?... Nonsense!... Not on your life, depositors rushing to withdraw their money indeed!... Who said that?... Um, er, all rumours, all rumours, don't you believe them. Now Mr. Chin, isn't the bank putting up a large new building next door to the hotel at this very moment?...Why are we building?... Why, naturally, when there's a flourishing market one likes to keep one's money on the move. Now don't worry! No question about the bank's reserve ... three days, just hold on for three days, for old times' sake, and you'll get every penny back.... Yes (*laughing*), Mr. Chin ... any special news about government bonds?... Ah, yes, so I hear, the market's looking up. A rise... haven't you bought a few?... Yes, yes....

FU-SHENG (*coming in through the door on the left*): Mrs. Li says Mr. Li will be here at once. (*Looking over his shoulder*) Mr. Pan's here, Mrs. Ku.

(*Mrs. Ku comes in, a fat woman of intolerable vulgarity. She is wearing a patterned gown, edged with a dazzling gold border, its arrestingly bright colours stretched taut against her body. Her walk brings to mind a miniature whale; her enormous buttocks pitch and sway so that it baffles the eye to follow their movements and one begins to wonder what else is wrapped inside that layer of clothing besides flesh and coarseness. Her face has its full share of wrinkles, but she conceals these deep furrows behind a wall built with paint and powder. She wears a permanent gay smile. This smile has various advantages: firstly, it makes her look more youthful; secondly, she believes that when she smiles she seems beautiful; thirdly, only when she smiles is her gold tooth revealed in all its dazzling splendour. So she bunches her mouth, eyes and nose together and smiles and smiles until one feels like weeping or vomiting. Her eyebrows are thin pencilled lines and the lobes of her ears are hung with diamond ear-rings that exude an aura of wealth; when she speaks it is always with excited gesticulations and considerable bodily movement, and then the jewels on her fingers — which resemble washerwomen's beetles—and her ear-rings, all flash and glitter until one's nerves are set on edge. She is really hale and hearty and as strong as an ox, yet strangely enough she is for ever ailing and at the slightest thing she will be overcome by dizziness, nausea and an interminable sequence of various aches and pains. But she also has her kittenish moments, for she thinks that the passage of the years has in no way diminished her girlhood charm, and when she is in one of these playful, mincing moods one really cannot help admiring the patience of Hu Sze, her latest gigolo — although sometimes even he turns his head away in disgust. Yet Mrs. Ku is in a world of her own, blissfully unconscious of the mocking smiles directed at her; for she is alive, always so happily, so youthfully alive, as one can see from the fact that last year she was — or so she said — just thirty, whereas this year she is suddenly twenty-eight, though she does have a daughter who is a university graduate. When Hu Sze is in a good mood he plays up to her and always says that she doesn't look anywhere near as old as that, and this encourages her to act more "naively" than ever when in the company of men.)*

(The sound of talk and laughter comes from the next room and when Mrs. Ku pushes open the door on the left and emerges the clatter of mahjong-tiles and the sound of noisy conversation becomes louder still. She seems to be escaping as she comes out, treading in a determined attempt at light-footed gracefulness, smiling and panting.)

MRS. KU (*facing back into the other room*): No, I'm quite
worn out, I couldn't possibly play another round. (*She
looks round and says gushingly, as if noticing Pan Yueh-
ting for the first time*) Why, Mr. Pan! What are you
doing in here all on your own?

PAN (*bowing*): Mrs. Ku. (*Pointing to the telephone, indicating that he has nearly finished.*)
(*Fu-sheng goes out through the centre door.*)

KU   (*nodding to him and turning to look in through the
doorway again*): No, Mr. Wang, no, I'm tired. No, Pai-lu,
it's my heart, if I play any more my old trouble will
be back again. (*She turns again and comes across to Pan
like a gust of wind, still addressing her remarks to the
other room.*) You must let me have a rest now. (*Dropping
ponderously on to a sofa*) I'm absolutely worn out.

PAN: ... Yes, all right, good-bye then, good-bye. (*Putting down the receiver*) Well, now, Mrs. Ku. ...

KU (*volubly*): Now that was very naughty of you, Mr.
Pan, leaving your game of mahjong to come in here all
alone to talk to someone on the phone! (*Lowering her
voice with exaggerated gravity*) You'd better be more
careful, when Pai-lu's just in there playing mahjong.
(*The would-be confidante*) It'll be safe with me, though:
who are you running after now? Who's this girl that
was ringing you up? I know all about you men; you
may be clever at making money and spending it, but
none of you understand a thing about love, what a great
and wonderful thing love is —

PAN: Mrs. Ku, you're the most sentimental woman in
the world!

KU (*gratified*):   That's the reason why I'm most tragic,
most distressed, most passionate, most helpless.

PAN: Well, why do you suddenly stop playing? There's
no need to be helpless when you can have a game of
mahjong.

KU (*suddenly reminded*):   Oh, yes, I'll have to trouble
you to pour me a glass of water, Mr. Pan. (*She sits down
and takes out some medicine from her hand-bag.*)

PAN (*pouring water*):   What's the trouble now?

KU: I must take some medicine.   Quickly, give me the
water.   I must take my medicine first before I do
anything else. (*She feels her heart and thumps herself
gently.*)

PAN (*handing her the water*):   Are you all right?   Pai-
lu's got all kinds of medicine here.

KU   (*swallowing the medicine*): That's a bit better!

PAN (*standing beside her*): If not you'd better take some
of Pai-lu's sleeping tablets and have a nap, how about
that?

KU (*making the most of it*):   No, that's not what I need,
I've a pain in my heart! The reason I stopped playing
just now was because I suddenly began thinking about
that ungrateful creature Hu Sze and it made my heart
start aching again.   You feel it if you don't believe me!

PAN (*reluctant to touch her*): All right, I believe you.

KU (*obstinately*):   Come on, feel!

PAN (*resignedly stretching out his hand*):   All right, then.
Feels all right to me.

KU (*put out*):   What do you mean, "all right"! I'm practically dead!   And my heart's thumping so hard it's
almost bursting.   I've been to one doctor after another
and they all said there was nothing wrong with me,
but I didn't believe it! Then I paid two hundred dollars
to be examined by the famous French doctor, M.
Ledoux, and he found out what was wrong with me
straight away: heart trouble.   It was no wonder that my
heart often pained me, when there was something wrong
with it all the time.   Feel it again if you don't believe
me and listen to the way it keeps pounding away. (*She
pulls at Pan's hand.*)

PAN (*having no alternative but to put his head down and listen*): All right, I will. (*Nodding his head repeatedly*) Yes, it is pounding away, isn't it?
(*Pai-lu comes in through the door on the left; she is in high spirits.*)

PAI-LU (*taken aback at seeing them and not knowing quite what to say*): Oh! You here, too, Yueh-ting?
(*Pan walks over to the table and lights a cigarette.*)

KU (*embarrassed*): What do you think of that? Mr. Pan giving me medical treatment!

PAI-LU: Is it your heart again? (*Looking round at the open door, through which still comes the sound of conversation and mahjong tiles*) Mr. Liu, I'll let you mahjong, even though you have got such a big hand. You must forgive me running off like this, Mrs. Li. If you want anything just ring for it. (*Seeing that Ta-sheng is not here*) Why, what's happened to that cousin of mine?

KU: Pai-lu, you don't mean that gentleman who starts frowning whenever he sees anyone, do you? You mustn't ask him here again! He gives me the creeps! (*She goes towards the window.*)

PAI-LU (*with a smile*): Yes — Ta-sheng! Ta-sheng!
(*Ta-sheng comes in through the door on the right.*)

TA-SHENG (*pausing in the doorway*): Oh, it's you. What did you want me for?

PAI-LU: Why don't you come out here and mix with the others?

TA-SHENG: I've been having a chat with the Shrimp. (*Happily*) A sweet child.

PAI-LU: And now how about coming out here for a chat with us. (*Going over to him*) Come and join us, don't be so stand-offish.

TA-SHENG (*glancing at Pan and Mrs. Ku*): No, I'd rather you let me talk to the girl. (*He turns and closes the door behind him.*)

PAI-LU: It's just hopeless trying to get him to do anything.

PAN: D'you know, Mrs. Ku, Hu Sze hasn't been in to the bank for work the last few days again.

KU: I had words with him and he went off in a huff. Don't take that too seriously, Mr. Pan, he — he —

PAN: All right, let's say no more about him. (*Standing beside Mrs. Ku at the window*) Look, they've already started work on the bank's new building. Once they've got the footings in they'll begin building straight away. In a good position like this we've only got to let it and we're sure of fifteen per cent interest at the very least. If the market improves slightly we'll make twenty or perhaps even thirty per cent.

KU: Listen to the wonderful schemes Mr. Pan's got, Pai-lu. Now what was it you were telling me, Mr. Pan? When the market is something-or-other and the economy is something else, you —what was it you said one should do?

PAN: I said when the market is critical and the economy unstable one should invest in property.

KU: That's it; you see, Pai-lu? If I don't spend money now on putting up buildings my market will become unstable, you see? So you were quite right when you had the idea of putting up this big building, Mr. Pan. Twenty per cent interest, that'll bring in two or three thousand dollars a month, very handy to help out with one's pocket-money.

(*Fu-sheng comes in.*)

FU-SHENG: Mr. Chang from the newspaper-office is here, sir.

PAI-LU: What's he want with you all of a sudden?

PAN: I asked him over so that I could ask him what's been happening these last few days.

FU-SHENG: Shall I ask him to come in?

PAN: No, you can take him along to room thirty-four.

FU-SHENG: Mrs. Tung's here, Miss, and Miss Liu, too.

PAI-LU: Take them all over the other side. They've come for mahjong. Say I'll be over at once.

FU-SHENG: Very good, Miss. (*He goes out.*)

PAN: Well, Mrs. Ku, that's settled then, I'll have your bank deposit transferred.

KU: I leave it all to you. If it's in your hands everything will be all right.

PAN: Good, I'll discuss it with you later.

PAI-LU: Just a moment, Yueh-ting. Remember what I told you.

PAN: What was that?

PAI-LU: About the Shrimp. I want to keep her as my adopted daughter. I want you to make it all right with Mr. Chin and put us in the clear.

PAN: All right, don't worry, I'll see to it. (*He goes out through the centre door.*)

PAI-LU: See how smooth-tongued he is?

KU (*she watches Pan jauntily depart, then looks round again and launches into another torrent of words*): I do admire you, Pai-lu! I really don't know how to do justice to you. You're a *chef d'oeuvre*! Charming, beautiful, romantic, voluptuous. Alone in a place like this, yet with friends everywhere. Mr. Pan, now, for instance: he doesn't support anybody, he says he only supports you. Mr. Pan's a good man, extremely able; to quote a modern phrase, he's a "unique unprecedented first class type." Can you find anyone to beat him, whether it's property or stocks or government bonds? That's why I've put my money in his hands for him to invest for me. And this is the man you've fallen for, you've hooked him, when you say yes he daren't say no, so I always say you're a girl with the most wonderful prospects.

PAI-LU (*lighting a cigarette*): It's not me that's hooked Pan, he comes here of his own free will, what can I do about it?

KU (*making an effort to please her*): Anyway, it's a case of "When Greek meets Greek."

PAI-LU (*deliberately flattering her*): You really are acquiring the gift of the gab these days. I always find it hard to think of something to say when I meet you.

KU (*preening herself*): Do you mean that?

PAI-LU: Of course I do.

KU: I feel the same myself. Ever since my old man passed away I seem to have had my eyes opened to things. I've suddenly become cleverer and I can put my tongue to anything. (*With a mixture of satisfaction and self-pity*) But what's the use of having a clever tongue? One still can't hold a man's heart with it. I'm now realizing for the first time, Pai-lu, that men have absolutely no conscience. However well you treat a man it's all wasted effort.

PAI-LU: Oh? What's Hu Sze been up to now?

KU (*with a long sigh*): Heaven only knows what he's doing! I haven't seen a thing of him for the past couple of days. I've phoned, written, gone to see him myself, but he's never in. What do you think of a man like that, after all the money I've spent on him and after lavishing my affection on him, and now look what he does: at the first little thing that upsets him he goes off and ignores me for days on end.

PAI-LU: In that case you've every right to ignore *him*, and save yourself a lot of bother.

KU: No . . . that's not the answer. I think that however modern a woman may be she must still have some regard for the old ideas of "submission and propriety." So no matter how badly Hu Sze treats me I shall always have a certain amount of affection for him.

PAI-LU: Congratulations, my dear!

KU (*taken aback*): What do you mean?

PAI-LU: Congratulations on becoming more respectable every day! Fancy you and Hu Sze embracing the idea of "submission and propriety"!

KU (*with an indignant flash of her eyes*): What! You don't imagine I'm a woman with no character or principles?

PAI-LU: But my dear Mrs. Ku, if you're going to start talking in terms of "submission and propriety" you'll have to ride in the bridal sedan-chair again and have a solemn and spectacular wedding, if you and Hu Sze are going to get married!

KU: You mean that Hu Sze and I should get married? (*Quickly shaking her head*) That would never do. If he treats me like this even before we're married, he'd treat me a lot worse afterwards — I'd be no better than an old cast-off shoe! And this modern-style marriage is just useless: if he changes his mind he's only got to go to a lawyer to get a divorce. Not like the time before when I married my late lamented: whatever he wanted to do about it I was still his wife! And a wife who'd been married in a bridal chair, too, so he had to behave himself and keep me as a lord and master should — and pay my bills. Couldn't he divorce me, you say? Get rid of his own lawful wedded wife? No fear of that! But now . . . (*gloomily*) ah. . . . Pai-lu, you're an intelligent girl, just think now, what's the point of getting married? What's the point of it?

PAI-LU (*with a sigh*): There's nothing in it either way. Though I've always thought that to make a lover into one's husband does seem a great pity.

KU (*not quite understanding Pai-lu, yet guessing the gist of her meaning*): That's just what I was trying to say! Having a meal together, for instance, or going to a dance: so long as two people aren't married they'll always enjoy it in a friendly atmosphere, but once they get married, humph — (*Her feelings getting the better of her, as if she can see Hu Sze already turned into a callous husband*) No, it can't be done, not if you talk till the cows come home. Hu Sze can say what he likes about it; if he proposes to me I shall refuse. And

besides, I'm afraid of him: once we were married he'd
show his true colours; and you know my eldest
daughter —

PAI-LU: You mean the young lady that's been to
university?

KU: Yes, that's the one.

PAI-LU: What about her?

KU (*launching into her second objection*): You know
what a free-and-easy sort of person I am, well, my
daughter's just the opposite. She's quite the intellectual, she's a Christian, goes in for charities, and gives
herself airs. But I'm not like that. Once I'd set my
heart on my Chiu, nothing else mattered to me but
him; now that I've set my heart on Hu Sze, all I live
for is Hu Sze. Funny, isn't it, my daughter being like
that when I'm like I am? Must be something to do
with heredity!

PAI-LU: But what's all that got to do with your getting
married?

KU: Oh, yes, I talk away till I forget what I was going
to say. (*Dropping her voice and speaking close to Pai-
lu's ear with animated gestures*) I tell you, my daughter's dead against Hu Sze — though of course I quite
understand why: she's afraid Hu Sze will spend all
my money for me; and also, if I married him, you see,
their ages would be . . . well, er, there wouldn't be
much difference between them, and you can imagine
how difficult it would be to know what she should call
him, and it would all be rather embarrassing for me!

PAI-LU (*yawning and trying to round off this tiresome
topic*): I don't see that you've got to be eternally
attached to Hu Sze when he treats you badly all the
time.

KU (*with a great show of pride*): But that's what love
does to you! Of course I do realize he's lazy and won't
change till the day he dies, so after much coaxing and
pleading I got Mr. Pan to find him a job. Mr. Pan said

that business was bad, but for my sake he dismissed quite a few people from the bank so that he could squeeze him in. And what does Hu Sze do? He says the salary's too low and the work doesn't interest him, and after going for a couple of days he's now stopped going in regularly. Lazy, good-for-nothing, helpless, — ah, poor boy, it's the way he's made! If I don't take him under my wing, who will? Ah, love! I've never understood what the word really meant till now.

PAI-LU (*mockingly*): No wonder you've become so clever.

KU: I tell you, love is when you willingly give him money to spend and don't mind how he squanders it — *that's* what love is! — Yes, that's love!

PAI-LU: That explains why I'm always hearing it said that love has its price.

KU: Yes, there's no doubt whatsoever about that. I'd like to get Mr. Pan to find him a job with a film company. Now, Pai-lu, seeing what good friends we are, couldn't you have a word with Mr. Pan for me? I really haven't the face to bother him again myself.

PAI-LU: What, you mean you want him to be a film-star?

KU (*fervently*): Yes, and what a hit he'd be! Don't you see, he's every inch a film-star! Physique, features, nose, eyes.

PAI-LU: But aren't you afraid of having other women run after him?

KU: No, that's one point on which I have complete faith in him. Whatever his faults he is at least devoted to me — he follows me about like a little dog. (*Suddenly realizing that this statement is slightly out of step with the facts*) Of course, he hasn't been to see me the last few days, but you can't blame him for that; you see, he asked me for three hundred dollars but I wouldn't let him have it, and he wanted me to buy a new car, a Chevrolet, but as I couldn't put my hand on the

money just at the moment I said no. Then he pro-
posed to me, but I turned him down again, so it's no
wonder that he's annoyed.

PAI-LU: So you want to find him a good position to
put him in a good humour again.

KU: I promised him this time that if only he'll become
a film-star I'll find some way to marry him. Now let
me tell you all about it; I've thought it all out: we're
sure to get some really big pictures in the papers, one
of me, one of Hu Sze, and one of both of us together,
and every day the papers will print the news of our
honeymoon. And also —

PAI-LU: But if you get married what about your
university-trained daughter? What are you going to
do about her?

KU (*confidently*): Oh, once Hu Sze's become a film-star
everything will be different. I'll get Hu Sze, as a film-
star, to go along to her charity fetes and so on and
sing a romantic song or two (*with a gesture of her
hand*), dance the hula, and she'll be delighted, you see
if she isn't!

PAI-LU: All right, my dear, I'll do it for you. You're
very clever, and you think of everything. I'll definitely see Mr. Pan about it and tomorrow he'll get him
into a film company. All right?

KU (*overcome with gratitude*): Thank you! Thank you!
There, didn't I say, Lulu, you were a unique *chef
d'oeuvre,* and I was absolutely right.
(*Fu-sheng comes in through the centre door with a
sheaf of bills in his hand.*)

FU-SHENG: Oh, I didn't realize you were here, Mrs.
Ku.

KU: What do you want?

FU-SHENG: It was Miss Chen I wanted to see. (*To
Pai-lu, handing her the bills*) Mr. Pan's paid the bills
that were due yesterday for you, Miss, and he told me
to bring them to you.

PAI-LU: Put them in the drawer for me.

FU-SHENG: Very good . . . er, but there are (*feeling in his pocket*) there are some more —

PAI-LU: More?

FU-SHENG: If you don't believe me I'll tell you what they are — (*He is about to recite them to her.*)

PAI-LU: Can't you see I've got a visitor?

FU-SHENG: Sorry, Miss.

(*Just as Fu-sheng is about to withdraw, Georgy Chang comes in through the door on the left. He is in evening dress and is carrying a top-hat, white gloves, a stick inlaid with ivory, and also a bouquet. He enters the room with a self-satisfied swagger.*)

GEORGY (*glowing with enthusiasm and heartiness*): Bonjour! Bonjour! I guessed you'd both be in here! (*Shaking hands*) Bonjour! Bonjour! (*He grips their hands tightly.*)

KU: 'Evening, Dr. Chang!

GEORGY: *Mademoiselle* Ku! (*Looking her up and down*) You really do look prettier every day. (*She is delighted and is about to reply when Georgy turns to Pai-lu.*)

GEORGY: *Tiens!* My little Lulu, this dress of yours is —

PAI-LU (*imitating his manner*): *Ravissante!*

GEORGY: Absolutely right! You're brilliant, you always know what I'm going to say. (*Turning to Fu-sheng*) By the way, er, *garcon!*

FU-SHENG: *Wee, m'shoor?*

GEORGY: Tell them in the next room that I won't be joining them for mahjong.

FU-SHENG: *Wee, m'shoor!* (*He goes out through the door on the left.*)

PAI-LU: Don't keep frisking around like that; sit down, why don't you?

GEORGY: *Bon, ma chérie.*

KU: Doctor Chang, I wish you wouldn't keep talking that foreign gibberish.

GEORGY: *Oh, je m'excuse, pardonnez-moi.* I'm terribly sorry, but you see I've really got out of the habit of speaking Chinese. I find it rather easier to express myself in French.

PAI-LU: Georgy, why are you all dressed up like this today?

GEORGY: Ah, you've no idea what a lot of things one gets caught for working in a government office. One day it's some ceremony or other, the next day it's a wedding one has to attend. Liu, the head of our department in the ministry, was married today, and I was his best man. Afterwards I suddenly thought of you and I felt I'd better come straight round to see you without waiting to change first. Oh, yes, I've brought you these flowers, to express my wish that you will always be as beautiful as you are today and also as a token of my remorse. The real reason I came into your suite last night was —

KU: What happened last night?

PAI-LU: That's all right.

GEORGY: All right, you say? Well, thank you, I always knew you were generous.

KU: Dr. Chang, you haven't been around with Hu Sze the last few days, have you?

GEORGY: Hu Sze? I saw him at the club the other day, wandering about with that dog of his again.

KU: The callous creature, he'd rather take his dog out than me.

GEORGY: Why, what's the matter, have you two fallen out again? Then what's he doing sitting outside in a car?

KU: What! You say he's outside?

GEORGY: Didn't you know? That's odd.

KU: Dr. Chang, nobody would think you'd had an education, honestly. Why didn't you tell me before?

GEORGY: I don't see that an education is any guarantee of being able to divine your wish to see Hu Sze.

KU: Well, I can't stop here arguing with you, I must be off. (*Going to the centre door in great haste, then turning round*) Oh, and Pai-lu, don't forget what I asked you to do for me. Remember to put in a word for me when you see Mr. Pan.

PAI-LU: All right.

KU: *Au revoir*, Dr. Chang! *Au 'voir!* (*She goes out.*)

GEORGY: Whew! Got rid of the old hag at last. (*Turning warmly to Pai-lu*) Pai-lu, I must tell you the good news.

PAI-LU: Good news? Your wife presented you with another son?

GEORGY (*with his usual self-satisfied wave of the hand*): Ah, you're impossible.

PAI-LU: Then you must have been promoted.

GEORGY: It amounts to much the same thing as promotion, what I have to tell you. This is it. (*Taking Pai-lu's hand and speaking intimately and happily*) Yesterday afternoon I got a divorce from my wife, a proper divorce!

PAI-LU: Oh, A divorce? But hasn't she given you three children? How can you go and divorce her as soon as you get back from abroad?

GEORGY: What do you mean? I paid her, I made her a proper settlement. What's the matter with you today? And now for my other piece of good news. (*Suddenly fixing her with a look of great tenderness*) Lulu, do you know why I came here last night?

PAI-LU (*mockingly*): Don't tell me you came to propose to me, too?

GEORGY (*taken aback*): *Oh là là! Juste ciel!* You must be God himself, the way you can guess what's going on in my mind!

PAI-LU (*alarmed*): What! You —

GEORGY: Now, Lulu, you must take pity on me, take pity on a man who has no one to love him. You must say yes.

PAI-LU: You mean that when you came here and made that scene last night (*with utter distaste*), and were sick all over my bed, you mean you'd come to propose to me?

GEORGY: That was because I was drunk.

PAI-LU: I'm well aware of that.

GEORGY: And that was because I was so overjoyed. I couldn't get over the realization that I was going to be the luckiest man in the world, because I knew you'd marry me. Lulu, I've now got a house in Kwangtung Road, I've some shares in the Ta Hsing Mines, and I've several tens of thousands in cash in the Ta Feng Bank, and of course you know that I'm still in the government service. Later on, if my luck holds, I shouldn't have the slightest difficulty in securing an income of three or four thousand dollars a month. In addition to all this, I didn't do so badly for myself while I was abroad: I'm a Ph.D., a B.Sc. in economics, and an M.A. in political science, and also —

PAI-LU (*shouting*): Ta-sheng, Ta-sheng, come out here. (*Ta-sheng appears from the bedroom on the right.*)

TA-SHENG (*seeing the two of them sitting together*): Oh, sorry. (*He turns to go.*)

PAI-LU: No, I called you, open the window, quickly.

TA-SHENG: What for?

PAI-LU: I want to breathe some fresh air. There's an awful fug in here all of a sudden.

TA-SHENG: Fug?

PAI-LU (*scathingly*): Why, yes, can't you smell it?

GEORGY (*looking at Ta-sheng*): I say, Pai-lu, aren't you going to introduce me? You're not being very polite, you know.

PAI-LU: Oh, haven't you met?

GEORGY (*looking at Ta-sheng*): Your face is familiar.
I've a feeling we've met before somewhere?

TA-SHENG: Have we?

GEORGY (*suddenly*): Why, of course, of course. We
have met before, we're old friends!

PAI-LU: Really? Where did you meet?

GEORGY: Yes, we're old friends. I remember now, a
couple of years ago it was, we came back together on
the same boat from Europe. (*Suddenly going up to
Ta-sheng and gripping him firmly by the hand, warmly*)
Jolly glad to see you again. Sit down, do. (*He turns
to get a cigar.*)

PAI-LU (*in a low voice*): What's the idea of all this?

TA-SHENG (*with a smile*): There's no telling what he's
after.

(*Li Shih-ching comes in from the left. He began as a
minor clerk in the Ta Feng Bank but his cunning and
a gift of flattery have now raised him to the position
of Pan Yueh-ting's secretary. He is a wizened little
man who strives to imitate the manner of the important
personage he imagines himself to be, yet he can never
disguise his seedy appearance and he is always fur-
tively watching the expression on people's faces and
smiling with a compliant sycophancy. When he as-
sumes a serious expression we discover on his forehead
a large number of wrinkles of long standing, one fine
furrow upon another, laden with all the humiliation,
poverty and distress that he has suffered in the course
of his life. When among all these "rich and noble"
personages that he so admires and envies he will often
feel pangs of shame at his own vulgarity, and so in
company, fearful of being despised, he will now and
then contrive to impress with hollow boasting, yet the
sudden remembrance of his home and family will make
him bow his head in mortified silence and withdrawal;
for he hates those above him yet he is obliged to be
subservient to them. There is nothing for it but to*

*swallow his indignant hatred and vent it on his poor
wife and children when he returns home. So much for
his odious yet pitiable character. His eyes are small
and ratlike, his hair sparse, his eyebrows so faintly
marked as to be almost invisible; dotted around his
mouth are a few isolated whiskers; he has a flat nose
and a short chin, and when he opens his mouth he
shows several blackened teeth; his voice is always shrill.
His short, lean figure is clad in a faded yellow, crackle-
patterned satin gown. Over this he wears a brand-new
black satin jacket. His entrance is heralded by the sound
of his patent-leather shoes, which are of the laceless
kind; though old and cracked they are highly polished.
His trousers are bound at the ankles.)*

LI: Good evening, Miss Chen! (*To Georgy*) Dr. Chang!
(*He bows.*)

GEORGY: Ah, you've come just right. Mr. Li, I'd like
you to meet an old friend of mine.

LI: Very pleased to, I'm sure.

GEORGY (*turning to Ta-sheng*): This is Mr. Li Shih-
ching, secretary at the Ta Feng Bank, Mr. Pan's right-
hand man.

LI: Not at all, not at all. And this gentleman is —

GEORGY: This is an old fellow-student of mine who
came back from Europe with me, Mr. — er, Mr. —

TA-SHENG: Fang.

GEORGY (*striking the side of his head*): Of course, what
a terrible memory I've got, yes, Fang, Mr. Fang.

LI: Pleased to meet you.

PAI-LU: You'd better watch out, Mr. Li. Mrs. Li's
looking for you, says she wants to see you about something.

LI: Is she? (*Smiling*) I don't see her having time to
speak to me. She's busy playing mahjong at the
moment.

PAI-LU: Still? She told me some time ago she wasn't going to play any more. How's she getting on, losing or winning?

LI: My wife's a poor player so of course she's losing, but she's keeping her losses down, only three or four hundred dollars, nothing —

PAI-LU (*saying it for him*): Nothing to speak of.

LI: You're a clever one, Miss Chen, the way you can take the words out of one's mouth. (*With an unnatural smile*) Really, though, it's a pleasure even to lose when we come here to your place for mahjong.

PAI-LU: Thanks for the compliment, though I really don't deserve it.

GEORGY: You haven't run into Mr. Pan, I suppose?

LI: I came here hoping to find him, as a matter of fact.

PAI-LU: He's probably in room thirty-four. Fu-sheng will be able to tell you.

LI: Thank you, Miss Chen. In that case I hope you don't mind if I leave you for a moment. Excuse me, Dr. Chang. Excuse me, Mr. Fang.

(*Just as Li, bowing and nodding, is about to depart, Mrs. Ku comes in through the centre door shepherding Hu Sze in front of her. He is just what one would expect one of his kind to be like: pale complexion, a high-bridged nose, thin lips, even white teeth, sleekly-combed hair, a tiny pencil-line moustache. When he happens to smile it is in an alluring manner which is enhanced by the romantic suggestiveness that never leaves his eyes. He never looks directly at one but gives one an oblique glance then quickly looks away as if he does not want to be seen looking at one, and this mannerism of his is universally held to be an endearing one. He does not often smile, and gives the impression of being rather sad; nor does he speak much, but when the occasional phrase or two escapes him one hears it with a sense of shock, for no one would imagine that such a handsome exterior could harbour*)

such a multitude of coarse, vulgar thoughts and feel-
ings. Yet he makes no attempt to disguise them since,
far from being aware of his vulgarity, he prides him-
self on being what many people praise him as being to
his face — "the most handsome boy in China." He is
for ever looking in a mirror, arranging his hair and
straightening his clothes; clothes are his second life,
sacred, inviolable treasures. At the moment he is in
European-style dress: black shirt, white silk tie, a violet
suit speckled with dots of various colours, cut with
fashionable bizarreness. In his hand is a short,
exquisitely-made cane with a glittering silver-coloured
chain.)

(As he comes in he wears an expression of easy-going
unconcern, and no shadow of any emotion ever passes
across his face; he shows neither alarm nor politeness,
nor does he bestow on the others so much as a nod
of greeting; he just walks in "mysteriously," as Mrs.
Ku puts it.)

LI: Good evening, Mrs. Ku. (*Familiarly*) Good evening,
Mr. Hu.

KU (*to Li*): Help me get him in.

LI: What's happened now?

HU SZE (*glancing at Mrs. Ku then turning unconcernedly
to Li*): Take no notice.

LI: You must excuse me, I have to see Mr. Pan. (*He
goes out.*)

KU (*petulantly, like an artless, unsophisticated girl, ob-
viously in imitation of Pai-lu*): Now you're to stay
with me! I won't have you looking at her! (*Pushing
Hu Sze into the room and speaking triumphantly, half
to Hu Sze and half to the others*) When I say you can't
look at her, you can't! Do you hear me?

HU SZE (*distastefully acquiescing*): All right, all right,
I heard you. Look what you've done now! (*With a
frown he jerks her hands from him and points at his
sleeve, which has had several creases crushed into it*

by the pressure of her large, pudgy hand.) Good
clothes ruined! *(He dusts himself down and straightens
his tie.)*

KU *(smiling uneasily, yet feeling obliged to be angry with
him since there are other people present)*: All this
fuss!

PAI-LU: Now what's all this about?

HU SZE: Nothing. *(Quick-wittedly taking Mrs. Ku
by the hand and smiling in a captivating manner)* What
a way to go on! *(He is going to say "What are you
making such a fuss about?" but changes his mind and
smooths back his sleek, glossy hair. Willy-nilly, they
smile at each other, and Mrs. Ku's good humour is
restored.)*

KU *(herself again, to Pai-lu)*: We do have fun, don't
we, quarrelling all day like this?

PAI-LU: You're like a couple of children, making scenes
like that in front of other people.

KU: But we *are* a couple of children! *(To Hu Sze)*
Aren't we? Now I ask you, why did you insist on
looking at that woman? It's not as if she was beautiful. Coarse, fat, common, no education —

HU SZE: Oh, forget it, why must you keep on about
it? *(He sits down without waiting to be asked, takes out
a handkerchief and wipes his face, then produces a
small mirror and looks at himself in it.)* I came in
when you told me to, didn't I? *(Suddenly seeing Georgy
and bowing)* Hullo, you're early, Professor.

GEORGY: Hullo, stranger, what have you been doing
with yourself lately?

HU SZE: Nothing to speak of. Fooled around in the
club, larked about with the girls around the dance-
halls, browned off, what a life!

KU: Humph, some low hussy's got her claws into you
again, I suppose.

HU SZE: There you go again! *(Indifferently and unhurriedly)* If you say so.

KU (*annoyed*): I didn't say one had for certain.

HU SZE (*still wearing the same expression of indifference*): That's all right then, isn't it?

(*Fu-sheng enters from the left.*)

FU-SHENG: The refreshments are ready, Miss, room fifty-one. Would you like to have a look at them first?

PAI-LU (*turning from talking with Ta-sheng*): All right, I'll be straight along.

FU-SHENG: Very good, Miss. (*He goes out through the door on the left.*)

PAI-LU: Hu Sze, have you met my new visitor? (*Hu Sze rises languidly.*) Mr. Fang, just arrived here, a cousin of mine. (*To Ta-sheng*) This is Hu Sze, the most handsome boy in China.

KU (*turning elatedly from talking to Georgy*): You mustn't praise him up so, he'll only go making my life a misery again.

PAI-LU: Well, you two be having a chat while I pop across to the other room and see that everything's all right.

(*She goes out at left*).

HU SZE (*unconsciously smoothing his hair again, he turns his head to consult the dressing mirror. After standing by Ta-sheng for a while without speaking, he suddenly blurts out*): Pleased to meet you; hope you'll keep an eye on my interests.

TA-SHENG (*not knowing what best to say*): Er — well —

HU SZE: Your face is familiar.

TA-SHENG: Is it?

HU SZE: How old are you?

TA-SHENG (*taken aback*): Eh?

HU SZE: You're quite good-looking, not bad at all. Tell you, you'll do well here. I say, Professor, don't you think Mr. Fang looks like my friend Huang Yun-chiu? (*He looks Ta-sheng up and down.*)

GEORGY: Huang Yun-chiu?

HU SZE: Yes, the one who takes the "staid female" parts at the Ta Wu Tai Opera.

TA-SHENG (*with distaste*): And I suppose you're the soubrette.

HU SZE: Good eyes you've got — well, actually, I'm not very good at it, though I do go in for it. I'm teaching Mrs. Ku, and Pai-lu's had lessons from me, too.

TA-SHENG (*to himself*): My God!

(*A pause.*)

HU SZE (*puzzled, then suddenly serious*):   Feel like something to eat, Professor?

GEORGY (*startled*): Eh? — No, I'm not hungry!

KU (*also at a loss to understand the reason for this unexpected question from Hu Sze*): You — you mean you're hungry?

HU SZE: I — er — (*glancing at Ta-sheng*) no (*shaking his head*), *I'm* not hungry.

(*A pause.*)

TA-SHENG (*looking at the three of them, with a sigh*): Excuse me, I think I'll go out for a walk.

GEORGY: But, Mr. Fang, you

TA-SHENG: You must excuse me.

(*Ta-sheng goes out through the centre door. The three of them watch him out, then exchange meaningful glances.*)

HU SZE: There's a stuck-up so-and-so for you!

KU: I suppose Pai-lu got bored and raked up the cranky creature from somewhere to amuse herself with, just for a lark.

GEORGY: It's funny, you know, I'm not so sure now that I have met him before.

HU SZE (*lighting a cigarette*): Professor, I can drive now.

KU: Yes, you haven't seen him drive yet, have you? He drives awfully fast.

HU SZE: Know what, Professor? I've been asked to join a film company. They want me as a *jeune pre-*

mier. So now I've started learning to ride, swim, dance, dress in European style. By the way, Professor, what do you think of my European outfit? Quite nice, don't you think?

GEORGY: Passable, passable. Though at the very least you should get your European suits made in Hongkong, and you shouldn't pay less than two hundred and seventy dollars for them.

HU SZE (*looking at Mrs. Ku*): Hear that? And you wanted me to have a job at the Ta Feng Bank for a monthly salary that wouldn't buy me one Western-style suit!

KU: Don't be so greedy. Li Shih-ching works hard from morn till night for only two hundred a month and he wouldn't be getting that if Pai-lu hadn't been kind enough to put in a word with Mr. Pan for him.

HU SZE: That's because he won't stand up for himself. Nobody could sell themselves as cheaply as that. (*Pai-lu comes in from the left.*)

PAI-LU (*standing in the doorway*): Come along, the refreshments are ready now. Come on in, everybody, and have something to eat. We're all old friends here today. (*Looking over her shoulder*) Look, Georgy's here, Miss Liu.

GEORGY (*catching sight of Miss Liu at a distance through the open door, he goes across, his hand already extended, exclaiming loudly*): Bonjour, bonjour, mademoiselle. (*With a wave of greeting*) — Ah, my dear Miss Liu. Don't get up. Let me come and keep you company. (*He goes in still talking loudly and an exchange of greetings is heard from within.*)

HU SZE (*unhurriedly hitching up his trousers and straightening his clothing, then turning to Mrs. Ku with his usual air of languid nonchalance*): Come on! I've been wanting something to eat ever since I came in.

KU (*staring at him*): Why couldn't you say so before? Don't wait about, then! (*She clatters forward.*)

HU SZE (*with a sideway glance at her, more slowly than ever*): Oh, you!

KU (*having now reached the door on the left she looks round and, seeing that Hu Sze still stands there, she extends a hand and beckons to him, smiling*): Come along now, Hu Sze.

HU SZE (*with a disdainful look, as if in triumph*): Tcha! (*With solid dignity he moves through the doorway on the left, giving Pai-lu an entrancing smile on the way.*)

PAI-LU (*looking all round*): Hullo, what's happened to Ta-sheng? (*Looking over her shoulder and suddenly seeing Mrs. Li behind her*) Why, Mrs. Li, aren't you having a bite to eat? . . . Oh, I see, please come in. (*Mrs. Li comes in, an emaciated woman with sedate movements and rather drably dressed. Her expression is gentle but suffused with sadness. Apart from a dusting of face-powder she is almost devoid of any artificial aids to beauty. She seems to have come here with great reluctance. As she talks with Pai-lu she is polite and very unsure of herself.*)

PAI-LU (*amicably*): you want to have a word with Mr. Li?

MRS. LI: Yes, Miss Chen.

PAI-LU (*ringing*): You *are* an affectionate couple, can't bear to be parted after all this time. I really do envy you. (*Fu-sheng comes in.*)

PAI-LU: Fu-sheng, go and ask Mr. Li to come. Tell him Mrs. Li wants a word with him.

FU-SHENG: Very good.

PAI-LU: Oh, and is Mr. Fang out there?

FU-SHENG: I haven't seen him.

PAI-LU: That'll be all, then. (*Fu-sheng goes out.*)

PAI-LU: Will you excuse me a moment, Mrs. Li, duty calls. (*Going towards the door on the right*) Ta-sheng, Ta-sheng!

(*The Shrimp comes out of Pai-lu's bedroom. She looks quite different from what she did twelve hours ago. She is wearing an old rose-purple dress of Pai-lu's, which is still too big for her, and one can tell at a glance that it is not her own. Her jet-black hair hangs down, her fair-complexioned cheeks are smeared with two patches of rouge. She looks slightly dazed, partly on account of her excessive weeping during the past few days and partly because of the strangeness and newness of her surroundings. She looks at Pai-lu and Mrs. Li without uttering a sound.*)

PAI-LU: Is Mr. Fang in there?

THE SHRIMP: Mr. Fang?

PAI-LU: The gentleman who was talking to you just now.

THE SHRIMP: Oh, him. No, he's not in there.

PAI-LU: He's gone off again, then. (*Suddenly, to the Shrimp*) Here, who told you to come out?

THE SHRIMP (*alarmed*): I — I came out because I heard you calling.

PAI-LU (*teasing her*): Have you already forgotten who came here last night, then?

THE SHRIMP (*immediately turning and going back through the doorway*): All right, Miss.

PAI-LU: Don't run away. (*The Shrimp backs into the room again.*) There's a window in there that opens on to a passage. Now, you must close it tightly, you hear?

THE SHRIMP: Yes, all right. (*She slips back into the bedroom.*)

(*Li Shih-ching comes in through the centre door.*)

PAI-LU: Ah, so there you are, Mr. Li. Your wife insists on seeing you. You really are a devoted couple.

LI (*politely keeping up the spirit of her bantering remark*): I tell you, Miss Chen, we're as much in love as ever we were. I get quite miserable if an hour passes without my wife whispering sweet nothings to me.

PAI-LU: Really? Then I'll leave you to talk to your hearts' content and I won't disturb you. (*She goes out through the door on the left.*)

LI (*he bows as he watches Pai-lu out of the door. There is a pause. Having looked all round he hardens his face and speaks in a severe voice*): Well, how did it go? Did you lose? Or did you win?

MRS. LI (*piteously*): Won't you let me go home now, Shih-ching?

LI: You lost again?

MRS. LI (*hanging her head*): Yes.

LI (*showing signs of agitation*): You mean you've lost the hundred and fifty dollars I gave you?

MRS. LI (*in a subdued voice*): I didn't lose all of it — though nearly all.

LI (*pausing, at a loss*): But how could you lose all that amount?

MRS. LI: I was nervous, afraid of losing, and that made my play worse than ever.

LI (*losing his temper*): Nervous? Hasn't everybody got an equal chance? What's there to be nervous about? You — you're like a child in arms!

MRS. LI (*unable to bear such unjust reproaches, tearfully*): I didn't want to play mahjong, but you would insist that I did. I didn't want to come, but you forced me to. I did as I was told, and came, and played for high stakes with all these wealthy people — and when I lose you go and — (*She weeps aloud.*)

LI (*looking at her and becoming more angry still*): Crying! That's all you're fit for! This is no place for you to start crying! Making a spectacle of yourself! Now stop crying. (*Impatiently*) I've plenty of money here, so let's have no more of this nonsense.

MRS. LI: I don't want any money.

LI: What do you want, then?

MRS. LI (*timidly*): I want to go home.

LI: Don't talk nonsense. Here's some more money. (*Taking out his wallet to comfort her*) Look, I've a hundred dollars here, look. Here's eighty to be going on with, how's that?

MRS. LI: Where did you get this?

LI: Never you mind.

MRS. LI (*suddenly*): Where's your fur coat?

LI: I left it at home, I'm not wearing it this evening.

MRS. LI (*catching sight of a slip of paper rolled in with the bank notes in his hand*): Shih-ching, what's that you've got there?

LI (*hurriedly*): It's a — (*But Mrs. Li has already snatched it from him.*)

MRS. LI (*looking at the slip of paper and handing it back to him*): You've pawned your fur coat again.

LI: Don't shout at the top of your voice like that!

MRS. LI: Oh, Shih-ching, what's the point!

LI (*crossly*): It's no concern of yours, I tell you, it's no concern of yours.

MRS. LI: Shih-ching, I've had enough. Now will you please let me go home. This is no place for us to come for an evening out. No respectable company, not a decent word spoken —

LI: What do you mean, no respectable company! Isn't Mr. Pan respectable? Look at the way he runs schools and builds poor-houses and provides factories — doesn't that show he's a good man?

MRS. LI: But haven't you seen the way he carries on with this Miss Chen —?

LI: Of course I have. That's because he likes her and because he's got plenty of money that he likes spending; what's all that got to do with respectability?

MRS. LI: Have it your own way, it's no affair of ours. (*Imploring him*) But surely you must see that on our small income we can't afford to come here to see this

Miss Chen? And keep company with all these wealthy people?

LI: How many times have I told you to keep that kind of remark for when you're at home, if you must make them? Don't come out with them here. Otherwise they might hear you and then you'd be a laughing-stock.

MRS. LI (*aggrieved*): I'm sure they all laugh at us a bit as it is.

LI (*indignantly*): What right have they to do that? We play mahjong with them and we can pay up as well as any of them! Don't we spend dollars by the hundred the same they do?

MRS. LI: But what's the point when we've got a houseful of children at home? There's Ying's schooling to be paid for, and Fang on the point of getting engaged, and Wu poorly again. And Mother hasn't a decent winter coat to her back. And yet you leave all these things aside so that we can come here and ruin ourselves playing mahjong with them, paying out a hundred dollars at a time, how — how *can* I go on playing?

LI (*hanging his head*): Stop talking about it.

MRS. LI: Isn't it hard enough for you to be a bank-clerk, working yourself to death all day and finding you can't make ends meet when you draw your salary at the end of the month, without making things worse by going around with your superiors, playing mahjong and keeping company with them? It doesn't matter if we can't afford to send the children to school, you must be sociable just the same, and when we can't pay the rent at the end of the month you must still mix with them. When one of the children is ill and we can't afford a good doctor, you still have to keep company —

LI (*bursting out*): Stop it! I won't have you talking like this! (*Bitterly*) Surely you can see what torture I go through all day? Don't you see that I'm haunted all the time by the thought of our poverty? I can never

stop cursing my bad luck in not having had a decent
father who could have brought me up in more comfortable circumstances, so that I could hold up my head
and look after myself better.   I'm not so bad as them,
the low crowd, you know that.   They're no better than
me.   They've no brains, no guts, no heart.   The only
way in which they're any different from me is that they
were born with money and social standing and I wasn't.
I tell you, there's no justice in the society we're living
in, no equality.   All this talk of morality and service
to the public is just a trick of theirs for deluding other
people.   If you work conscientiously you'll only die
a pauper.   All you can do is to burn your boats and
fight them in the hope that one day you'll come out
on top!

MRS. LI: You're so busy fighting, Shih-ching, that you
don't give a thought to our own children.   What's going
to become of them?

LI (*with a sigh*):   Children!   Humph, if it wasn't for our
poor children you don't imagine I'd be swallowing my
sense of shame and dragging you along to a place like
this, do you?   What's Chen Pai-lu, anyway?   Something between a dancing-girl, a prostitute and a con-
cubine, but not quite any one of them.   Low and cheap!
But this old fool takes a fancy to her, and the old fool's
rolling in money, so I have to call her "Miss" and
agree with everything she says.   The way it looks to
you, though, I'm going down on my knees to them as
if they were my ancestors.   Su-chen, you don't realize
how I loathe myself sometimes for giving up my self-
respect and lowering myself to flatter them.   Here am
I, a man past forty, bowing and scraping all the time
and mixing with these bastards and even with such
low trash as that Hu Sze — every one of them I have
to flatter and be sociable with.   Me, Li Shih-ching, a
real man, me — (*He drops his head and falls silent.*)

MRS. LI. Now, Shih-ching, you mustn't upset yourself
about it, you mustn't be so downhearted. I know how
you feel after all you've had to put up with.

LI: *I'm* not downhearted. (*He raises his head and says
indignantly*) Humph, I'll be even with them yet, I'll
have my revenge. I'm going to be as hard as a stone,
no room for sentiment at all, no more feeling sorry for
people. In the twenty years I've worked here, look
at the shabby way I've been treated. But I'll get somewhere sooner or later, and then I'll let them have it
with a vengeance. You'll see, I'll be back on my feet
soon.

(*Pan Yueh-ting comes in through the centre door.*)

PAN: Ah, Shih-ching! You're back, then.

LI (*deferentially*): I've been here some time. I understood you were passing the time of day with someone
from the newspaper office so I didn't like to send someone to invite you over.

PAN: Were you busy with Mrs. Li?

LI: No, no, we've finished what we were saying. (*To
Mrs. Li*) You'd better go back to your game of mahjong.
(*Mrs. Li goes out left.*)

LI: Is there any news from the newspaper office about
any special change in the situation?

PAN: It would be no concern of yours if there were;
have you bought the government bonds I told you to
buy?

LI: Yes, two million altogether, this month's issue.

PAN: What sort of price did you get them for?

LI: Seven seventy-five.

PAN: And what happened after you'd bought?

LI: Not a very favourable reaction, I'm afraid. What
with rumours flying and money tight and share-prices
dropping all the time and holders of government bonds
offloading them; but you have to go and —

PAN: I have to go and buy them up.

LI: On the expectation of a rise, of course.

PAN: Well, you don't imagine it'd be in the hope of a
    fall!

LI (*with great earnestness*): In the ordinary way, Mr.
    Pan, there's not much risk attached to stocking up
    with bonds: at a pinch you can always cash them and
    buy them back later. But this is a special situation,
    with prices going down and down all the time. If they
    should settle there's always hope that they'll come up
    again and then you'll make a packet. Though that's
    something we've no control over.

PAN (*taking a cigar*): How do you know you can trust
    these rumours?

LI (*smiling deferentially*): Ah, I see, you mean they're
    being deliberately put about? By the bears, who want
    to start covering?

PAN: Though rumours don't bother me. I think I should
    be able to tell a piece of reliable information when I
    hear it, after all the years I've been going in for gov-
    ernment bonds.

LI (*ingratiatingly*): Yet Mr. Chin always has the best
    inside information, and I hear he's not buying at all.
    Also —

PAN (*annoyed*): It's always best, Mr. Li, to mind one's
    own business. What you're told to do at the bank
    you must do, and what you're not told to do you must
    keep out of and not start asking questions. That's the
    rule at the bank.

LI (*greatly put out by this rebuff, yet doing his utmost
    to control himself*): Of course, Mr. Pan, but I was
    only mentioning it to remind you.

PAN: The bank's affairs are not open to discussion.

LI: Very well, sir.

PAN: You've been to see Mr. Chin, then?

LI: Yes. I mentioned the matter of the new building
    that the bank's putting up. He said he didn't see how
    the bank could afford it just now. And then he went
    on to talk about the difficult state of the market and

the way land prices are falling, and he said that as the
building's only just been started, it would be advisable
to stop work on it at once.

PAN: But didn't you tell him the contract for the building's been signed and the earnest-money paid?

LI: Of course, I told him the job had been taken by a
foreign contractor and that there was no question of
asking for our money back, which meant that for the
moment it would be just impossible to free Mr. Chin's
deposit with us, so could he give us a couple of days'
grace.

PAN: What did he say to that?

LI: He thought for a moment then said "We'll see,"
though I should say from the expression on his face
that he'll most likely change his mind.

PAN: The so-and-so! Not a spark of decency in him!

LI (*with a surreptitious glance at Pan*): Oh, and he also
asked me whether all the bank's properties had been
mortgaged yet.

PAN: What! He said *that*?

LI: Yes, I thought it was a bit of a cheek.

PAN: What did you tell him?

LI: Naturally I told him that nothing of the sort had
happened. (*He pauses. After another surreptitious
glance at Pan he plucks up courage.*) Though I am
aware that every inch of the bank's properties *have*
been mortgaged.

PAN (*taken aback*): You — who told you they'd been
mortgaged?

LI (*looking up*): Isn't it a fact, sir, that a few months
ago you mortgaged the bank's last piece of property,
extending from the lane of Changsing to Huangjen?

PAN: Nonsense. Who told you that?

LI: And didn't you mortgage it all to the Yu Hwa Company?

PAN: Oh, er. (*Pacing a few steps*) Now, Shih-ching, where did you get this information from? (*Sitting down*) You mean to say that people know about this?

LI (*realizing he has put his finger on his opponent's vulnerable spot*): No, no, set your mind at rest, nobody knows but me. No one else could see the contract you signed.

PAN: You've seen the contract? Where?

LI: In the drawer of your desk.

PAN: How dare you —

LI: The fact is (*with a crafty smile*), I was rather puzzled by what was going on in the bank, suddenly putting up a large building and buying government bonds at the same time, and one day when you were busy seeing a client I took the opportunity to have a look in your drawer. (*Smiling*) I do realize, though, that it was a bit of a liberty to take.

PAN (*after staring at him blankly for a while*): No, no, that's all right. I wouldn't call it a liberty. (*With an uneasy smile*) Good thing to keep an eye on each other, you know. Now, won't you sit down? We must talk this over.

LI: That's very kind of you, sir.

PAN: Not at all, sit down, make yourself at home. (*Sitting down*) Now that you know about this matter, you understand, of course, that it's all very confidential and not on any account to be divulged to anyone, otherwise it's going to put the bank in an awkward position.

LI: Yes indeed. I'm aware that there have been quite a number of large withdrawals recently.

PAN: Right, then, so we sink or swim together. We'll have to help each other and combine forces to keep the bank on its feet. Just lately there have been a lot of rumours circulating about the bank and casting doubts on the sufficiency of our reserves.

LI: Whereas in actual fact not only are our reserves insufficient, but we're even short of ready cash. Isn't that the case, for example, with Mr. Chin, wanting to make this withdrawal?

PAN (*uneasily*): But, Shih-ching —

LI (*cutting him short*): All the same, sir, since you've been putting it about that the bank's making money and since you announced your plan for erecting a large new building for the bank, the general rush to withdraw deposits has quietened down a bit.

PAN: You're not slow, you've seen the method in my madness. So this building must go up. It doesn't matter when it's going to be finished: all that matters is that the fact that we can afford to have it done shows that the bank's got plenty of reserves and that it's on a firm footing.

LI: This thing about making money, though: the bank staff know we're not.

PAN: Hence the vital necessity for keeping quiet about the mortgages and about Mr. Chin's withdrawal. Just at the moment either of these facts leaking out could start a panic, so you must be very careful.

LI: Naturally I shall be careful. All the time I've worked under you I've been very discreet, and there's no reason why I should fail you now.

PAN: I've another scheme up my sleeve. If we can make a bit on these government bonds, it'll tide us over for the present. Once we're out of the wood I'll see to it that your loyalty is properly rewarded.

LI: You can always rely on me, sir. I — er — I recently heard that your assistant Mr. Chang is to be transferred.

PAN (*hesitantly*): Er, yes, my assistant, yes, he is. Well, if you don't think that position too low, I'm quite prepared to help you.

LI: Thank you, sir, thank you. Don't worry, you can always rely on me to do my utmost for you.

PAN: That's that, then. Good. — By the way, have you brought the list of redundancies?

LI: Yes.

PAN: About how much will we save by these cuts?

LI: Only about five hundred dollars a month.

PAN: Every little helps. Did you make a deduction from the wages on the building site last pay-day?

LI: Yes, two hundred dollars, I've got it with me.

PAN: As much as that?

LI: It's not all that much really. I only deducted a mere ten cents for each labourer.

PAN: All right, we'll deal with it later. (*He takes a couple of steps towards the door on the left, then suddenly looks round.*) Oh yes, I knew there was something else: when you saw Mr. Chin did you mention the matter of that little girl last night?

LI: Yes, I said Miss Chen had taken a great fancy to the child, so would he spare us any embarrassment.

PAN: What did he say?

LI: He shook his head and pretended he didn't know anything about it.

PAN: Curse him. Pretending not to know. Friendship doesn't mean a thing to him. — Oh, well, let him have his way.

LI: I'll do that, sir.

(*Pan goes out.*)

(*Suddenly the telephone rings.*)

LI (*picking up the receiver*): Hullo, who's that? Oh! I see, Mr. Chang from the newspaper office. You want to speak to Mr. Pan? He's not here . . . it's me, Shih-ching. You can tell me, it'll be all the same. I see. What? Mr. Chin's buying the same issue as us? How much? Three million! That's odd, yes . . . yes, no wonder our manager's been buying them too! . . . Yes, you're right there, government bonds are practically Mr. Chin's own private property, all the manipulation's done by him. . . . Yes, I agree, it looks like a rise after all . . . right you are . . . I'll go and tell the manager straight away. Good-bye, Mr. Chang. Good-bye!

(He puts down the receiver, pauses a moment, then turns to go out by the door on the left.)

(Huang Hsing-san comes in through the centre door.)

HUANG *(timidly)*: Mr. — Mr. Li.

LI: You again. What do you think you're doing coming round after me here?

HUANG *(weakly)*: Nothing else I could do. I've a whole family at home with nothing to eat.

LI *(coldly)*: You think you'll get something to eat by coming here? This is a hotel, not a soup-kitchen.

HUANG: Mr. Li, I've pawned everything that can be pawned. I've nowhere to turn, otherwise I'd hardly dare come here again bothering you.

LI *(with detestation)*: What am I, a relative of yours? Or an old friend? Or am I in your debt? Just what do you think you're doing, following me around wherever I go?

HUANG *(with a wry smile, bleakly)*: You're quite right, I've no such claims on you, but Mr. Li, while I was working at the bank I only cost you thirteen dollars a month. If you take my job away from me, where am I to get another? By turning me out now, the bank's as good as forbidding me to go on living.

LI *(with annoyance and distaste)*: Who's forbidding you to go on living? What you're saying in effect is that the bank should never dismiss anyone. The bank hasn't undertaken to feed you for the rest of your life, if that's what you imagine!

HUANG *(twisting his scarf in his fingers)*: No, no, I don't mean that, Mr. Li, I —I realize the bank's treated me well; I'm not being ungrateful. But . . . you haven't seen the houseful of lively children at home that I have to find food for every day. Now that the bank's dismissed me I've no money coming in, we've no rice left in the house and they're all crying out that they're hungry. The rent's six weeks in arrears, so very soon they won't even have a roof over their heads.

(*Brokenly*) Mr. Li, you haven't seen what a crowd of children I've got. I've nowhere to turn.

LI (*cold*): Whose fault is that?

HUANG: Whose fault? Mr. Li, when I was at the bank I never once did a job badly. I was always off to work at the crack of dawn and I never got home till late at night. I worked from morn till night, Mr. Li —

LI (*losing patience*): All right, all right, I know you've been a conscientious worker, content with your lot and not giving any trouble. But surely you realize that there's a depression, an economic crisis? It's not as if I hadn't warned you. I've told you time and again that the bank would be cutting down on staff and salaries. You can't say I didn't warn you!

HUANG (*hesitantly*): But Mr. Li, isn't the bank putting up a large new building at the moment? And they're still taking on people in the bank, new people.

LI: That's no concern of yours! It's all part of the bank's policy, to improve business. As for taking on new people after dismissing you, I should have thought that after all the years you've been in business you'd have learnt that much at least about the way of the world.

HUANG: Yes, I — I have, Mr. Li. (*Pitifully*) I realize I've got no one behind me to give me a push forward.

LI: There you are, then.

HUANG: But I always thought: Providence doesn't let down a man who does his best, so if I work hard I may be able to make up for this shortcoming.

LI: And that's the reason the bank's kept you on for four or five years. If you hadn't worked hard you wouldn't have stayed on this long.

HUANG (*pleading*): Mr. Li, I beg of you, help me just this once. Won't you *please* have a word with Mr. Pan, and ask him to take me back? I'll do anything, willingly, even if it means extra work, extra tiredness, even if I have to work myself to death.

LI: You're a pest. You don't imagine the manager is going to bother with your troubles? There's only one thing wrong with people like you: you always attach too much importance to yourselves. In other words, you're just plain selfish. How do you imagine a busy man like Mr. Pan is going to find time for your petty problems? Though I can't make it out: how can you have been working for us all these years without getting together at least a small amount of savings?

HUANG (*with a wry smile*): Savings? What, on thirteen dollars a month with a large family to feed? Savings?

LI: I don't mean out of your salary. You naturally couldn't make anything extra on your salary. But—in other ways, surely you made yourself something on the side?

HUANG: No, Mr. Li, I always kept my conscience clear.

LI: I mean — surely you made something for yourself out of buying stationery?

HUANG: Never, my conscience would never allow it. You can ask the chief clerk, Mr. Liu.

LI: Humph! You must be a fool if you're as particular as that about your conscience! No wonder you're in such a pitiful state now. All right, now you can get out.

HUANG (*in a panic*): But Mr. Li —

LI: If anything turns up we can reconsider the matter. (*Waving him away*) At the moment I can do nothing for you. Now go.

HUANG: Mr. Li, you can't —

LI: I tell you: if you come trotting around after me like a little dog again, following me everywhere I go, you'll find I won't treat you so politely next time.

HUANG: Then you mean there's absolutely no hope at all?

LI: Get moving! There'll be a whole lot of ladies coming in here in a minute, and if they find you coming to see me here it's going to be very awkward.

HUANG: All right, then. (*Hanging his head, his eyes filled with tears*) Mr. Li, I really must apologize for treating you like this. (*With a wry smile*) Coming and bothering you all the time. I'll go now.

LI: Go on, then.

HUANG (*he heaves a long sigh and begins to move away but after a couple of steps he suddenly turns and comes back. He says miserably*): But where can I go? Where can I go? My home's broken up. I'll swallow my pride and tell you: my wife's left me. We had nothing to eat and she couldn't bear our miserable existence any longer, so she ran off with somebody else. There are three children at home waiting for me to take them home something to eat. At the moment I've only twenty cents in my pocket and I'm also ill (*coughing*), all day long I'm coughing. Mr. Li, where can I go? Where can I go?

LI (*sorry for him, but also despising him for his feebleness*): Go where you like. Though I'd like you to know that it's not that I don't *want* to help you out with some money, but I'm afraid I can't make a precedent of your case.

HUANG: I'm not asking you for money, all I'm asking you to do is to be so kind as to give me a job. I must live, for my children's sake!

LI (*thinking a moment, then looking disdainfully at Huang*): The fact is there are plenty of jobs about if only you're willing to take them.

HUANG (*a spark of hope reviving in him*): You mean that?

LI: First, you could go rickshaw-pulling.

HUANG (*disappointed*): I — I could never manage it. (*Coughing*) You know I'm ill. The doctor says the lung on this side is already (*coughing*) — unreliable.

LI: I see, in that case you can always go begging —

HUANG (*flushing, uneasy*): Mr. Li, I *have* had an education, you know. I just couldn't —

LI: You just couldn't bring yourself to accost people, is that it? Well, there's still another way left open to you, an extremely easy way that will give you what you want without any fuss: you can go into other people's houses and (*seeing Huang's lips moving soundlessly*) — that's right, you've got it.

HUANG: What, you mean — (*with trembling lips*) you mean I should turn to — (*One sees his lips move but no words are audible.*)

LI: Say it out loud, what are you afraid of? "Theft!" "Theft!" Why not, after all? When the rich can grab money by the fistful from other people's pockets it surely doesn't require very much courage to steal!

HUANG: To tell you the truth, Mr. Li, I have been driven to thinking of it. (*Terrified*) But I'm afraid to, I'm afraid, I could never bring myself to it.

LI (*exasperated*): Well, if you haven't even got the guts to steal, what do you expect me to do about it? You've neither influential relatives nor influential friends, nor have you any outstanding abilities. So there you are: I tell you to beg, but your pride gets in the way; I tell you to pull a rickshaw, but you haven't the strength; I tell you to steal, but you haven't the guts. You keep belly-aching about conscience and altruism and morality and expect to be able to keep a wife and family on honesty and humility; why, if you can't even provide for a wife, you poor useless thing, you're not fit to have a family! I tell you, this world is not meant for people like you. (*Pointing out of the window*) See that tall building out there? That's a department store, thirteen storeys high. I think that would be the best way out for you.

HUANG (*not understanding*): But how, Mr. Li?

LI (*going up to Huang*): How? (*With a mephistophelean smile*) I'll tell you. You climb up, storey after storey. And when you get to the very top you get over the railings and stand on the edge. All you have to do then is to take one step forward, out into space. It may be rather frightening for a moment, but it will only last a second, only one second, and then you will be out of your misery, with no more worries about finding food and clothing.

HUANG (*dumbfounded, his voice almost inaudibly low*): But Mr. Li, you mean I should commit — (*suddenly in a tragic voice*) no, no, I mustn't die, Mr. Li, I must stay alive! For my children's sake, for my motherless children I must stay alive! My Wang, my little Yun, my — yes, I had thought of it. But Mr. Li, you must keep me alive! (*Grasping Li's hand*) You must help me, just this once, I mustn't die, I mustn't die no matter how hard it becomes to live, I must stay alive at all costs! (*He coughs.*)

(*The door on the left opens wide. Through it comes the laughter of Mrs. Ku, Hu Sze, Georgy Chang and the others. Pan Yueh-ting half appears, speaking back into the other room: "Carry on playing, I'll be straight back."*)

LI (*jerking Huang's hand away*): Let go of me. There's somebody coming in, so behave yourself.

(*Huang can only stand there, leaning against the wall, as Pan Yueh-ting comes in.*)

PAN: Hullo?

HUANG: Sir!

PAN: Shih-ching, who is this? What's he doing here?

HUANG: My name's Huang, sir. I'm a clerk at the bank.

LI: He's one of those who've just been dismissed.

PAN: What do you mean by coming here? (*To Li*) Who let him in?

LI: I don't know how he found his way in.

HUANG (*going up to Pan, piteously*): Be good to me, sir. If you must dismiss someone don't let it be me. I've got three children, I must have a job. I'm going down on my bended knees to you, sir, you must let me go on living.

PAN: I've never heard of such a thing! How dare you
come here asking me for a job, you — (*furiously*) get
out!

HUANG: But sir—

LI: Get up! Get up! Go on, get out of it! (*Sending
him sprawling with a shove*) If you carry on making
a nuisance of yourself I'll get somebody in to kick you
out.

(*Huang looks from Li to Pan.*)

PAN: Out, get out, and quick! I've never heard of
such a thing!

HUANG: All right, I'll get up, I'll get up, you needn't
hit me. (*Slowly getting to his feet*) So you're not going
to let me stay alive. You! (*Pointing at Pan*) You
(*pointing at Li*), neither of you will let me stay alive.
(*Sobbing hysterically, halfway between tears and
laughter*) Oh, it's not fair! You're a couple of heartless monsters. Only thirteen dollars a month you paid
me, though with all the deductions you made all I
actually got was ten dollars twenty-five. And for this
miserable ten twenty-five I spent all day writing, all
day crouched over a desk writing for you; I had to
write on and on without a chance to look up or draw
breath; I wrote from morn till night; with a cold sweat
on my back and the words blurring before my eyes I
had to keep writing, on and on; through wind and rain
I came to the bank to write for you! (*With a gesture*)
Five years! Mr. Pan! Look at me, see what's left of
me after five years of that! (*Thumping his chest with
his hands*) A walking skeleton, a man at death's door!
I tell you both, my left lung's gone, yes, the doctor
says it's rotted away! (*In a shrill voice, past caring
now*) I tell you, I'm at death's door, I'm going on my
knees to you, for the sake of my poor children. Let
me go on writing for you, writing on and on, hour after
hour — give me a chance to keep body and soul
together. Give me a few more ten twenty-fives in ex-

change for my worthless life. But you won't! You won't! You want to make money for yourselves, you must cut down your staff, so it has to be me! (*Brokenly*) But what do you want my miserable ten dollars twenty-five for? It's not as if I've been taking your money for nothing: you've had my life in exchange for it! And now I won't even have a few more ten twenty-fives from you, and so I shall die. (*Bitterly*) There's not a spark of decency in either of you, the way you've treated me — you're thieves, you're robbers, you're devils! You haven't as much humanity between you as the beasts of the field —

PAN: You're mad, you scoundrel! Get out of my sight this minute!

HUANG (*weeping*): It's you that's mad! I'm not afraid of you now! I'm not afraid of you any longer! (*Seizing Pan's clothing*) I've had more than I can bear and I'm determined to kill —

PAN (*swiftly punching Huang in the chest*): What! (*Huang at once falls to the floor.*)
(*A pause.*)

LI: He means he's going to kill himself, sir. — A man like that wouldn't hurt a fly.

PAN (*dusting his hands*): It doesn't matter now, he's fainted. Fu-sheng! Fu-sheng!
(*Fu-sheng comes in.*)

PAN: Get him out of here. Put him in another room and tell Mr. Chin's men to massage him till he comes round, then give him three dollars and tell him to clear out.

FU-SHENG: Very good, sir. (*He drags Huang out of the room.*)

LI: Mr. Chang rang through.

PAN: What about?

LI: Mr. Chin's bought three million of the same bonds as you.

PAN (*his face lighting up with delight*):   I knew it! That means he's expecting a rise.

LI: So long as the information's reliable, and Mr. Chin is buying, then of course he's expecting a rise.

PAN (*pacing up and down*):   It must be right, it must be.

(*The door on the left opens wide and Georgy Chang, Hu Sze, Mrs. Ku and Pai-lu come in and stand in the doorway, while other female visitors can be heard talking and laughing beyond.*)

GEORGY (*in the highest of spirits, a cigar in his hand*): — So I maintain that it's hard to live in China, nowhere where you can live in comfort.   You've only to look at my Jacky now, (*to Hu Sze*) — the hunting dog I brought back from America with me — even finding the beef for him to eat is a great problem for me every day.   Dirty, neither clean nor nourishing, and fifty cents a pound, why he just can't eat it.   I tell you, I put four pounds of raw beef in front of him every day (*putting his nose forward and sniffing*), he sniffs as it then goes off with his tail between his legs, won't even look at it.   Just think, even the animals in China are feeling the pinch, not to speak of human beings! And as for people like us, well!   (*He shakes his head and shrugs, and everyone bursts out laughing.*)

(*Outside, Ta-sheng is heard shouting "Shrimp! Shrimp!"*)

PAI-LU: I say, listen, what's Ta-sheng shouting about?

(*Ta-sheng bursts into the room.*)

TA-SHENG: The Shrimp!   Have you seen the Shrimp, Chu-chun?

PAI-LU: But she's in there, isn't she?

TA-SHENG (*disbelievingly*):   In there?   (*He hurries into the room on the right, shouting.*)   Shrimp!   Shrimp!

KU: What's all this about?

(*Ta-sheng reappears.*)

TA-SHENG: No, she's not in there, she's gone. As I
was coming up the stairs just now I saw her go down
in the lift with two or three men. I just caught a
glimpse of her and then she disappeared. I could hardly
believe my eyes, but when I come and look I find she
has been taken away after all. (*Picking up his hat*)
Good-bye, I'm going to look for her.
(*He hurries out.*)

PAI-LU (*going across to Pan*): See what happens when
I ask you to do something for me, Yueh-ting! (*Suddenly*) Wait for me, Ta-sheng! I'm coming with you!
(*She throws an overcoat round her shoulders and goes
towards the door.*)

PAN: Pai-lu!
(*She hurries out, ignoring him.*)

KU (*becoming caught up in the excitement herself*):
Really, what is all this about? (*Clutching at Hu Sze*)
Hu Sze!

HU SZE (*shaking her off with calm deliberation*): Look
at you! (*He begins looking in his mirror again.*)

—QUICK CURTAIN—

Act III

One night a week later at about twelve o'clock, in the third-class brothel called the Precious Harmony, where a babel of hawkers' cries, shrill conversation, women's curses, and all the sounds of busy whoredom boil and bubble in a hell-brew of noise.

The main entrance is always plastered with such New Year couplets as "Southern women are beauties from birth; Northerners are rouged by Nature," while across the lintel of the centre door there is always a horizontal inscription, such as "A Paradise for Lovers" or "The Wonderland of the Peach-blossom Spring." In front of the entrance stand two or three women winking and ogling, with significant gestures, at the loungers walking by, who stare with pretended preoccupation at the dirt-blackened red glossy paper tariff of charges on the wall (on it are scrawled four items: "Short time . . . cents; all night . . . dollars . . . ; shared room . . . cents; light entertainment . . . cents"), then tease the women with some unrestrained back-chat until the latter, thinking there is a chance of doing business, go forward to ask them inside, whereupon the loungers move off roaring with laughter. This back-street houses like an anthill these so-called "dregs of humanity," fighting a continuous battle with hunger, but they differ from other pinch-bellied wretches in that whereas the others can wince and frown at the pangs of hunger these women must always smile.

Inside, the brothel is dovecotted with rows of tiny rooms, and when business is good there is a continuous stream of men of all descriptions coming and going through this catacomb: small business men, electricians, petty clerks, stewards on shore-leave, messengers from foreign business houses, and some hulking great fellows in short jackets with an ostentatious display of buttons, which are undone to reveal their chests. One may come and go as one pleases in the courtyard, and when one goes in through the main entrance a lame man shouts "Out front! Visitors!" A small copper bell on a rope begins to ring and out of the various little dovecots there emerge one after the other a number of creatures without a trace of natural colour, at once mechanically clustering together into a knot, sometimes laughing, noisy, turbulent. The "visitors" have of course been shown inside by now. Their eyeballs roll this way and that as they look about them. Now an attendant shouts in a shrill, ear-splitting voice: "Come and see the visitors!" Fat and thin, they come forward in turn, as the attendant calls out their professional names, to walk quickly past before the "visitors" with smiles and sidelong glances. Those standing behind begin whispering and chattering with their heads together, until one of the creatures, with every appearance of delight, is chosen by a visitor, and then the rest of them return whence they came.

Surprisingly enough, for all the amorous conversation and the various excesses that are taking place inside the little dovecots, the courtyard outside is a continuous babel of noise: girl street-singers, beggars going from doorway to doorway singing shulaipao, *tramps chanting snatches of Peking opera, gramophone-players, vendors of fruit, peanuts and chestnuts, "lucky dip" men, hoarse, raucous paper-boys, two-stringed fiddle-players offering their services as accompanists to those wishing to sing, sellers of hot "tea-eggs" . . . the lowest buskers of every description, and hawkers pushing their wares, each one of them going along the lines of little windows bawling at the top of their voices, sometimes even lifting aside*

the door-curtains and going in, insisting that the "visitors" do business with them.

But the audience can only see one of the little dovecots — a long, narrow, dark and dingy little room.

There are two doors in the back wall of the room, one
on the left and one on the right, both opening on to the
front courtyard, each with an impossibly tattered blue
curtain over it to keep out draughts. Between the two
doors is a curtain hanging from a wire strung across at
right angles to the wall; when this is drawn across it
divides the room into two. When there are too many
visitors who are strangers to one another they are put
on either side of the curtain, so that they can still drink
tea and talk without disturbing one another; in this way
one poor creature can look after two lots of visitors at
once, thus economizing on space and saving her legs, and
also saving on lighting and heating. At the moment the
curtain, the upper part of it discoloured by yellow spots
and the bottom of it torn and jagged, is pushed back
against the wall instead of being drawn across the room,
which means of course that the occupant is not too busy
just now.

On the right is a wooden bed spread with an old thin
sheet and with the quilts piled at the foot. The right-
centre wall over the bed is plastered with pictures —
"Piglet's Wedding," "New Year Festivities," "Chubby
Child Picking a Lotus-flower" — and a number of cigarette advertisements depicting attractive women. By the
door is the character fu (happiness) in red placed upside
down which means "happiness is here." Near the bed
is a rickety old dressing-table on which are a cracked
washing-bowl and one or two small decorated bowls.
Under the bed several pairs of embroidered shoes lie
scattered in disorder; beside the bed are several chairs.

On the left by the wall stands a square table with a
couple of chairs by it; on it are set out an incomplete
tea-service and a battered round tin holding cigarettes.

On the right there is also a pair of hanging scrolls mottled with black smudges; the left-hand one reads "Her beauty is that of a Hsi Shih reborn" and the right-hand one "Her face is the face of a Tiao Chan come into the world again." Fitted in between the two scrolls is a dressing-mirror which gives a grotesquely distorted reflection; across the top of it is the inscription "A thousand pieces of gold for one of her smiles." There are also one or two deck-chairs scattered about the room.

To the left and to the right there are windows, each covered with a small red curtain; under the left window there is an iron stove which is on the point of going out. By the table stands a stove burning coal-dust briquettes, of which there is a heap under the table. Above the small door to an inner room on the left hangs a picture-frame enclosing the inscription "Hua Tsui-hsi," which would seem to be the professional name of the girl occupying the room.

When the curtain rises, Tsui-hsi is standing in the doorway, her back to the audience, holding aside the door-curtain and looking out. She is about thirty years old, a creature degraded and ill-used almost to the point of utter numbness. She is not at all good-looking, rather plump, her face heavily powdered, her eyes ringed with rouge spread on her eyelids, her hair hanging down over her shoulders, her forehead purposely pinched into purple patches running straight across like a string of petals and the sides of her temples pinched even more horrifyingly purple. She is wearing a rust-coloured wadded gown with a velvet sleeveless jacket over it, cloth shoes, and cotton-padded trousers bound at the ankles with black satin ribbons. She is holding the stub of a cigarette in her right hand, and from time to time she blows the ash off it and puts it to her lips. Now and then she scratches at her hair with the same hand.

She is laughing and calling out, as if having a conversation with someone outside.

The various sounds outside mingle in a confused medley of noise.

FIRST VOICE (*shrilly*): Oranges and bananas! Peanuts and chestnuts!

SECOND VOICE (*weakly*): Gramophone!

A LITTLE GIRL'S VOICE (*to the lilting, swerving sound of a two-stringed instrument*): Sing you a song!
(*The sound of men's and women's laughter, beatings, curses.*)

TSUI-HSI (*waving out of the door*): See you tomorrow, Fatty! Cheerio, Mr. Chang! Cheerio, Mr. Chen!

THE VOICES OF "FATTY" AND HIS FRIENDS (*muffled*): See you tomorrow, Tsui-hsi.

TSUI-HSI (*suddenly standing on tiptoe and raising her voice*): Fatty, keep yourself well wrapped up this cold weather, don't get frozen.

FATTY'S VOICE (*as he comes back and takes Tsui-hsi by the hand, speaking with affection yet with a note of banter*): Why, my dear Tsui-hsi, you love me more than my wife does! Come here, my love! (*As he says this he seems to give Tsui-hsi a sudden tug.*)

TSUI-HSI (*almost falling through the curtain in the doorway into Fatty's arms, she holds on to the doorpost for support and pulls herself up straight again, then pushes Fatty's hand away and says laughing and panting for breath*): You wicked rascal, Fatty, leave go of me. You'd better go home and see your wife for a bit of tit instead of pestering me!

ONE OF FATTY'S FRIENDS (*smacking his lips and speaking with a note of admiration to tease them*): I say, I say, look at these two youngsters, raring to go. Here, Fatty, you'd better stay here if the women are going to keep getting you worked up like this.

FATTY'S VOICE (*playing the infatuated fool*): He's right, my love, I'll stay here with you.

TSUI-HSI (*well aware that they are teasing her, and pushing them away*): Go on, off you go, out! Stop playing the fool. Come again tomorrow, Fatty, and make sure you *do* come! And you two gentlemen come with him!

THE MEN'S VOICES (*insincerely*): All right, Tsui-hsi, we'll be here.

THE VOICE OF A PAPER-BOY (*deep and hoarse*): Paper, evening paper! Whole family takes opium. Read all about it. Clerk jumps in the river. Read all about it.

TSUI-HSI (*she turns her head to look at the paper-boy, and when she looks round again she finds the Fatty and his companions are almost out of the gate. She suddenly shouts*): Fatty, make sure you come tomorrow! If you don't come tomorrow, your children will be born without holes in their backsides, d'you hear? (*She laughs.*)

(*She swings round, throws away her cigarette-end, clears her throat and goes to the square table on the left. She picks up the notes left by Fatty, counts them, then puts them back on the table with a sigh.*)

TSUI-HSI (*sitting down on the chair by the table*): God, it gets worse every day. I don't know how I can stick at this game a minute longer. (*She picks up a cigarette-end from the table and lights it. Outside can be heard all kinds of hawkers' street-cries. She turns towards the little room on the left.*) Little Tsui! Little Tsui! (*She goes to the doorway and pulls aside the curtain.*) Aren't you going to get up, Little Tsui? If you don't do as you're told — (*suddenly*) oh, I can't waste my time on you, you headstrong child.

(*A short, squat figure comes in, wearing a short jacket and carrying a jug. His thick lips curl back to reveal two large jutting front teeth. When he speaks, the sounds emerge blurred and breathy between his parted lips, and he also has a slight stammer. He goes to the table, sets down the jug on it, counts the notes and looks suspiciously at Tsui-hsi.)*

TSUI-HSI: Why the look, Shun-tze?

SHUN-TZE: Is this what the f—f—fat fellow left?

TSUI-HSI: Why, don't you think it's enough?   He's saving his dollars for his funeral, that's his trouble.

SHUN-TZE (*shaking his head*):   Are you ha — handing it all over?

TSUI-HSI: Why not?   The boss must have one dollar a day, you know.

SHUN-TZE: But wha—what are you going to eat with?

TSUI-HSI: Eat?   Don't make me laugh!   I have to live on air and grow fat on it. (*She goes to the stove burning coal-dust briquettes and warms herself.*)

SHUN-TZE (*turning round, as if reluctant to speak*): Yo-yo-your old man's here a-a-again.

TSUI-HSI: He's wasting his time.   I've got no money for him, even if he killed me.   If business had been good I'd be the last to grudge sending a dollar home, or even two or three, to make things easier for the family.   He needn't keep on coming here to see me. (*Lowering her head in thought, then, suddenly*) By God, when I first came to work here business was so brisk that I'd see two dozen visitors a day, and even you, Shun-tze, didn't you use to pick up nearly a dollar a day in my room?   Humph (*shaking her head*), it's no good, I'm past it now.

(Under the window there is a beggar singing shulaipao *and playing the "seven castanets" — the "five swingers" in his right hand and two large bamboo castanets in his left, which go "di-di-da, di-di-da, di-di-da, di-di-da, di-di-da.")*

THE BEGGAR (*with a prefactory cough, singing in a quick, lively voice*):

  "Oh, we rattle 'em fast and we rattle 'em slow,
  As up to the Hall of Beauties we go.
  Two scrolls hang there beside the door,

Writ by a master's hand, I'm sure.
And what do they say?
'All day the cups go from hand to hand,
And every night brings a different man.'
(Di-di-da, di-di-da, di-di-da-di-da-di-da.)
With a one and a two and a three,
You make less on your back than you do on the tea,
So it's tea for the ugly ones, the handsome boys for
  me.
The ladies treat their guests in style,
Melon-seeds and sugar-plums all the while.
Then it's 'Come here, my darling, come here, my
  sweet,
Come to my arms and I'll give you a treat.'"

THE BEGGAR'S VOICE (*going back to his feeble speaking voice*): Mr. Manager, ladies, have pity on a poor blind man.

TSUI-HSI: Go on, get out of it. Don't come round here with your caterwauling, we've no money. (*Taking the cigarette-end from her lips and throwing it out of the door*) There, there's a fag-end for your trouble. (*Seeing the beggar pick it up*) Would you believe it! Things are looking up these days: when a blind man sees a fag-end now, he's only got to reach out and pick it up!

THE BEGGAR (*grinning broadly*): Ah, but I'm only blind in one eye. See you later, ma'am.

SHUN-TZE: Your — your chap wants you to take the kid and go back home to him.

TSUI-HSI (*clearing her throat contemptuously*): Go back home? What, in this weather, so that I can freeze to death? At least the kid won't die if it stays here. Tell the cripple I'm busy here with visitors and that I won't be out till later. I suppose he's out standing at the gate?

SHUN-TZE: I asked him in but he wouldn't come. He says he — he doesn't want to lose face.

TSUI-HSI: Humph! What face has he got left to lose,
I should like to know, when he can't even support his
wife, and after sharing me with other men all these
years!

SHUN-TZE (*wiping down the table*): Where's the new
girl that's just moved in?

TSUI-HSI: Little Tsui, you mean? She's in there.

SHUN-TZE (*lowering his voice*): I reckon Black San'll
be back soon.

TSUI-HSI (*with a sigh*): I tell you, she hasn't done a
single job all evening. When Black San gets back he'll
thrash her within an inch of her life, you mark my
words.

(*The Shrimp now comes out slowly from the room on
the left.*)

THE SHRIMP (*now quite changed, bitterly and slowly,
without so much as a "humph!"*): He can thrash me
to death if he likes, I've only got to die once.

TSUI-HSI (*taken aback*): Why, Little Tsui, what's come
over you?

SHUN-TZE: You've ch-ch-changed your tune, Little
Tsui. Aren't you afraid of Black San any more?

(*The Shrimp wipes away a tear but says nothing. She
is now wearing a lined blue jacket and black trousers
and her harrowing experiences of the past few days
have given her a different look. The expression of
childish naivety that she once had has now been
masked by one of seriousness and gloom.*)

SHUN-TZE: You're a queer kid, won't do business when
you can, can't do anything but cry all day. If you don't
powder your face, and put on a dab of rouge, how —
how do you think you're going to get any customer?

(*The Shrimp sits down by the table with her head bent,
fidgeting with her clothes and ignoring him.*)

TSUI-HSI (*to Shun-tze*): Take no notice of her, the
kid's a born rebel. You can talk to her till you're blue

in the face. Might as well talk to a brick wall. Dumb
as they make 'em.

*(Shun-tze goes out through the front door on the left,
taking the jug with him.)*

(A pause.)

THE SHRIMP: *Will* Black San be back soon?

TSUI-HSI: Soon enough, don't you worry! Now listen,
three days you've been here, without finding yourself
a single customer. And every one of these three days
Black San's made your life a misery. Don't give
yourself airs because you came here from a big hotel
with a better class of customer. When you come here
you have to behave yourself and do as everyone else
does. You don't imagine that bitch's bastard of a
Black San is going to let you off, do you, when he finds
you've gone another day without doing any business?

THE SHRIMP: There's a limit to what you can take.

TSUI-HSI: A limit? Not in this game there isn't. I'm
telling you, we're not together in this because we're
friends or sisters: it was our fate that brought us together here. You come out of the blue and find yourself
sharing my room, where you've been for the last three
days: that's your fate. I'm not blowing my own
trumpet, now, but when I first came into this business
I was queen of them all and I saw shining silver dollars
by the thousand. But it's like pearls: when they get
old and tarnished they lose their value. When you get
on in years you can't stand the pace and you end up in
a place like this. You've just got to stick it or else go
under. I tell you, my Little Tsui, once you get into a
place like this you can give up all ideas of respectability. God knows, you're smothered in men all the
time. Whoever comes to you, no matter who he is,
friend or stranger, if he says bed then bed it must be;
it's off with your trousers and let him do as he likes
with you. What bloody chance have you got of keeping
your respectability when you have to go on like that?

THE SHRIMP (*almost in tears again*):   But — but —

TSUI-HSI: But what?   Men — there's not a decent one among them.   They're all sex-mad, every one of them that comes here.   They play the fool, laughing and joking all the time, but when the moneyed gentlemen have finished amusing themselves, after they've had their fun and gone, we're each left with our own heart-aches, and in the quiet of the night we think to ourselves: every one of us had a father and a mother. Every one of us was some fond mother's darling when we were babies.   Every one of us has to have children of our own when we grow up, and look after a family. Humph!   We're all human beings, none of us was born as low as we've had to sink.   We're not earning a living in this murderous hole because we want to! (*Her head sinks forward as if she is going to cry.*)

THE SHRIMP (*taking out a handkerchief and offering it to her*):   Here . . . wipe your eyes.

TSUI-HSI: I'm not crying. (*With a sigh*) My crying days are over, long ago.   It's not that I haven't got feelings the same as anybody else, but I'm getting old and weary. Sooner or later I'll have worked myself to death to keep my family alive, and then I'll be bundled up in a piece of matting and buried out in the fields, and then it'll all be over.   But you're young and you've still got plenty to look forward to. If you can stick it for a few years until you find yourself a husband, you can turn your back on all this and have a family and make a comfortable life for yourself.   You don't want to be so obstinate with Black San: give in to him a bit, otherwise you'll only be making things harder for yourself. When we come here we're stuck here, and the worst that can happen to us is to die.   Where else is there to go? What sense is there in keeping on getting yourself thrashed by Black San, the queer's brat?   You know what they say about women like us: "Resentment in our hearts but a smile on our lips."   No need to show your hand.

When he says something nice to you, listen to him;
when he says something nasty, let it run off you like
water off a duck's back, just pretend he hasn't said a
thing. That's the only way to keep sane.

THE SHRIMP: I — I just couldn't stand it.

TSUI-HSI: Come off it, of course you can stand it. The
sun goes down in the west today and tomorrow it'll
get up in the east the same as always. Only somebody
with no guts would moan about not being able to stand
it. My God (*sighing*), people are a poor feeble lot,
afraid of any sort of suffering, but when it comes to
the pinch they *have* to put up with it. You can't just
stop living for a day!

THE VOICE OF A PAPER-BOY: Paper, evening paper,
read all about it. Clerk jumps in the river. Paper,
evening paper. Whole family takes opium. Read all
about it.

THE SHRIMP: Listen!

THE VOICE (*fading into the distance*): Paper, clerk
jumps in the river.

TSUI-HSI: Don't waste your time listening to that. You
know the saying: "Spend all your time listening to
the crickets and the crops'll never get planted." Now
get your face done up, ready to see any customers.
(*The crying of a waking child comes from the small
door on the left.*)

THE SHRIMP: Your baby's awake. You'd better go
in and feed him.

TSUI-HSI: Yes. (*She goes out*).
(*Street cries can be heard outside; from beyond the
door comes the crying of the child and Tsui-hsi's
soothing murmurs as she rocks it to sleep.*)
(*The Shrimp sits down on the bed without a word.*)
(*From next door comes the sound of a woman singing
lasciviously to the accompaniment of a four-stringed
Chinese fiddle. The song goes:*)

"You called me your little sweetheart,
sleepless until the dawn.
When morning came,
you left my bed.

Lover,
I can't bear to lose you;
one night together,
and I love you for ever more.

I sit in my room
while the lonely hours drag by,
thinking of you
in love with another girl.

Lover,
I can't bear to lose you;
my heartless love,
how can you be so cruel?"

After a few bars she stops and there is a roar of laughter from herself and the men with her.)
(The Shrimp throws herself face downwards on the bed and begins to sob. Shun-tze comes in through the front door on the left and goes over to her.)

SHUN-TZE (*looking at her*): Here — here, look, Little Tsui, if you go on like this you'll only be. . . .
(The Shrimp looks up at him.)

SHUN-TZE (*with a sigh*): Little Tsui, what — what do you intend to do?

THE SHRIMP: Nothing.

SHUN-TZE (*his thick lips curling back*): Why must you be so obstinate? We're not living on our own farm where all we need to do is to work hard and then we can earn enough to keep body and soul together. You —you can't be fussy when you come to a place like this. Just look at — at the way Black San's b — b — been knocking you about these three days.

THE SHRIMP (*suddenly*): Why did my dad have to go
and be crushed to death by a girder?

SHUN-TZE: If your dad was alive he'd still be dirt
under people's feet; who'd take any notice of him?
What could he do, a miserable footings-rammer?

THE SHRIMP (*pursuing her memories*): Well, perhaps I
wouldn't have sunk to this. He was more of a man than
Black San will ever be.   He was tall and strong, and if
he'd seen Black San putting me in a brothel he'd have
hit him once and killed him. My dad was a decent
man.

SHUN-TZE (*his eyes shifting from side to side*): Yes,
but — it's all over and done with now; he's dead.

THE SHRIMP (*in a low voice*): Yes, he's dead. I saw it
with my own eyes, I saw the girder — I saw it crush
him to death. (*Flinging herself face down on the bed
again*) Oh, Dad! (*Sobbing*) Dad!

SHUN-TZE: Now don't be a little idiot. You'd be better employed trying to pick up a customer instead of
crying for your dad.

THE SHRIMP (*in tears*): Who says I don't want to pick
up a — a customer? But if I go out to see the visitors,
they — they'll all — they'll say I'm too young, and
then they won't pick me, so what can I do?

(*Shun-tze sits down at the table.*)

(*Outside the window is someone giving a stylish ren-
dering of "Chin Chiung Under Escort" to the accompaniment of castanets made of pieces of broken
crockery:*

"*Here I stand before you in the street;
good people, hear my tale.
No highwayman am I, nor armed robber chief,
nor am I an outlaw come to surrender.
Yang Lin accused me of collaborating with robbers,
and so I am exiled to Tengchow.*

> 'Tis hard to leave the prefect who has shown me
>   such great kindness,
> hard to leave my fellow officials in the yamen,
> hard to leave all my neighbours and friends,
> hardest of all to leave my white-haired mother.
> My mother and her son are truly as one flesh,
> and my banishment of a thousand miles will cause
>   her to grieve.
> With the red sun sinking behind the western hills,
> I ask my escorts to find me a lodging for the night.")

THE SINGER (*giving a loud chiming clang on his castanets at the end of his song, then resuming his usual mournful voice*): Wealthy sirs, have pity on a poor man. I'm far from home and stranded in a strange city. It's bitter cold, so spare me the price of a bed, wealthy sirs.

THE SHRIMP: What's the time?

SHUN-TZE: Gone twelve.

THE SHRIMP: There won't be any more people coming now, will there?

SHUN-TZE: Well, the lights'll be going off soon, of course. Though there's no telling: we might get a great crowd of visitors come bursting in.

THE SHRIMP (*looking at Shun-tze for a moment and sighing*): I'd better hang on, though it shouldn't be for long.

SHUN-TZE (*not understanding*): Humph, you can't very well go to bed until all the visitors have gone. Though you never know, any minute there might be somebody coming in to stay all night, and if he takes a fancy to you and decides to spend the night with you it'll mean you'll be going to bed a bit earlier.

A SHRILL VOICE OUTSIDE: Out front! Over this way, sir. Clear a room there!

SHUN-TZE: Visitors. (*Towards the inner room*) Visitors, Tsui-hsi. (*He goes out with the jug and Tsui-hsi comes in from the room on the left.*)

TSUI-HSI: What are you doing just sitting here on your own?

THE SHRIMP (*wiping away her tears*): Did the baby go to sleep?

TSUI-HSI: Yes, he's asleep.

THE SHRILL VOICE OUTSIDE: Come and see the visitors!

TSUI-HSI (*to the Shrimp*): Go on, see what you can do. If you get yourself a nice visitor for all night you'll save yourself getting another thrashing tonight.

(The Shrimp dazedly stands up.)

THE SHRILL VOICE: Come and see the visitors! Come out, all of you, back and front! Come and see the visitors!

(The Shrimp is shepherded out by Tsui-hsi.)

THE SHRILL VOICE (*pausing after each girl's name*): Precious Orchid, Golden Cassia, Turquoise Jade, Cherry-apple, Black Jade. . . .

(The sound of a small bell.)

ANOTHER VOICE: Clear a room. Clear a room. This way, gentlemen. Come and sit down in here.

(Shun-tze lifts the door-curtain aside and shows Fu-sheng and Hu Sze into the room. Hu Sze is wearing a fur overcoat, a sleeveless purple woollen jacket with a wrap-over front, a high-collared lined gown of crackle-patterned grey satin, patterned silk stockings, black satin shoes; he wears his melon-shaped cap askew and an inch or so of white shirt-cuff is visible; he comes in with a carefree air. Fu-sheng is also in high spirits, his face shining and glowing; he is wearing an old sheepskin gown beneath which the edges of his uniform are visible, so that one can deduce that he has hurriedly thrown on the gown and slipped out of the hotel. As they come in the door, Hu Sze looks all round and takes out a handkerchief, which he holds over his nose.)

FU-SHENG: What's the matter?

HU SZE: Heck of a smell in here. (*As he says this he sits down slantwise on the corner of the table.*)

FU-SHENG (*wiping at the table with his hand*): Watch out for your clothes.

HU SZE (*springing up and dusting his overcoat*): Blast! What a godforsaken hole.

FU-SHENG (*smooth-tongued*): Well, I've brought you here, Mr. Hu, and now I must be getting back to the hotel.

HU SZE (*grabbing hold of him*): Oh no, you don't. You must stay here with me and keep me company.

FU-SHENG: Have a heart, sir, it's a busy time at the hotel just now. Mr. Pan's in the middle of entertaining guests and I must be back looking after them.

HU SZE: But surely you got somebody else on the staff to stand in for you?

FU-SHENG: No, nobody else knows I've come over here with you. In case Mrs. Ku finds out about it, let me make it quite clear now that you came on your own.

HU SZE: Don't worry, I'll keep your name out of it.

FU-SHENG: All right, then, I'll stay a while, but I'll have to be getting back soon.

HU SZE: I'll be going back soon, too.

SHUN-TZE (*to Fu-sheng*): You haven't been to see us for a long time, Mr. Wang. Your usual girl's been shifted, so I'm afraid it'll have to be someone else.

FU-SHENG: No, it's not for me, it's for Mr. Hu here. (*Indicating Hu Sze*) Mr. Hu's dropped in to see what it's like and amuse himself.

SHUN-TZE: Shall I fetch a few out for you to have a look at, then?

HU SZE (*very much the man of the world*): Yes, let's see a few of them for a start.

SHUN-TZE: Very good, Mr. Hu. (*Going out*) Visitors, come and see the visitors!

FU-SHENG: So after going to all that trouble to get me to come here and show you this Shrimp, you now turn round and don't want her after all.

HU SZE (*with a withering glance*): And why not? If you pay your money without looking a few of them over, you're not getting your money's worth, you idiot. We can still pick the Shrimp later on to entertain us. (*Shun-tze pulls aside the curtain over the front doorway on the right, though he does not come in.*)

SHUN-TZE (*to the prostitutes outside*): Come inside here.
(*Hu Sze and Fu-sheng go and stand in the doorway, looking out.*)

ANOTHER VOICE: Come and see the visitors! Come out all of you, back and front! Jade Orchid! (*A prostitute flits past the doorway.*)

HU SZE (*sticking out his tongue with disapproval*): What an old hag.

THE OTHER VOICE (*rattling the names off quickly*): Torquoise Jade! Golden Cassia! Cherry-apple! Black Jade! (*As their names are called the prostitutes flit past the doorway, laughing and giggling among themselves.*)

HU SZE (*making various gestures and comments as each creature parades before him, as if inspecting cattle*): No good, no good at all; that one'd be all right if she wasn't so skinny. (*With a leer at Fu-sheng*) There's a nice fat sow! They get worse and worse! — Nice name that one's got, pity she's got no looks. (*Fu-sheng is playing the yes-man to these remarks.*)

THE VOICE: Tsui-hsi!

HU SZE (*looking at Tsui-hsi*): Bet she's a goer.

THE VOICE: Little Tsui.

FU-SHENG (*to Hu Sze, in an undertone*): That's her, that's the girl.

THE VOICE: Feng-o! Tiny! Yueh-ching!

SHUN-TZE (*to Hu Sze*): That's the lot, sir. Apart from the ones that are ill or on leave, that's the lot. .

HU SZE (*to Shun-tze*):   Tsui-hsi and Little Tsui, are they in together?

SHUN-TZE: Yes, they're in the same room.

HU SZE: We'll have those two, then.

SHUN-TZE: Miss Tsui-hsi and Little Tsui. (*Tsui-hsi and the Shrimp come in. Shun-tze goes out.*)

TSUI-HSI (*in a very experienced manner*):   Which of you two gentlemen am I waiting on?

HU SZE (*pointing to himself*):   Me.

TSUI-HSI: And my young friend?   (*Indicating the Shrimp.*)

HU SZE (*pointing to himself*):   Also me.

TSUI-HSI (*tittering*):   Is that quite the thing?

FU-SHENG: What's wrong with it?
(*The Shrimp recognizes Fu-sheng.*)

TSUI-HSI (*to Hu Sze*):   And what's your name, sir?

HU SZE: Hu, Hu Sze.

TSUI-HSI (*to Hu Sze*):   Pleased to meet you, Mr. Hu. (*Indicating Fu-sheng*) Won't you introduce me to your friend?

HU SZE: Oh, this is Mr. Wang Pa [1]

FU-SHENG: The Wang part's all right, but he's pulling your leg about the Pa part!
(*Shun-tze comes in with a jug. He produces a packet of melon-seeds from his pocket, opens it and puts it on a metal dish on the table, then waits for an attendant to bring in the hot face-towels.*)

TSUI-HSI (*offering the melon-seeds*): Mr. Hu? Mr. Wang? Now, aren't you going to take your overcoat off, Mr. Hu?

HU SZE: No, I don't like getting cold. (*He dusts the covers on the bed with a handkerchief before sitting down on it.*)

TSUI-HSI (*to the Shrimp*):   Well, don't just stand there. (*Turning to Hu Sze*) You'll have to make allowances

---

[1] This is a pun. "Wang Pa" can either mean "Wang, the eighth son" or else "cuckold."

for her, Mr. Hu. She's a beginner, she's only been in the business a few days.

FU-SHENG (*answering for Hu Sze*): Don't worry about that.

HU SZE (*taking the Shrimp by the hand*): Let's have a look at you. Not bad at all, no wonder Mr. Chin took a fancy to her.

FU-SHENG (*pointing to himself*): Recognize me?

THE SHRIMP (*gritting her teeth*): I'd recognize you if you were ground to dust.

FU-SHENG (*amused*): Listen to that! She's only been here three days and she's learnt to talk tough already!

HU SZE (*appraising her*): The kid's got a good head on her shoulders all right! Dress her up a bit — I could choose her clothes myself, come to that — and take her out to the Jockey Club, and in less than three days she'd be the talk of the town.

FU-SHENG: Very nice, too, but do you think she deserves such a stroke of good luck?

HU SZE: But . . . (*suddenly, to the Shrimp*) wasn't it you that hit Mr. Chin?
(*The Shrimp throws Fu-sheng a look of hatred, then lowers her head and does not say a word.*)

TSUI-HSI: Mr. Hu's speaking to you, you ninny.
(*The Shrimp stands there like a statue.*)

FU-SHENG: Look at her, like a block of wood.

HU SZE (*lighting a cigarette*): I can't make it out, a little shrimp like that daring to go for Mr. Chin.

FU-SHENG: What can you expect from a yokel? Don't know what's good for them, not to the end of their days. Born cantankerous, the lot of them. Just think, to have Mr. Chin take a fancy to her, the chance of a lifetime. She could have had whatever she'd asked for. She could have lived on the fat of the land, all the clothes she wanted, a gay time, parties, the lot. But no, by God (*looking round at the Shrimp*), she's got it into her head that she's going to stay a virgin,

won't sell at any price. (*Pointing at the Shrimp*) I
suppose your father's a bank manager? Or does he
run a gold mine? The big money comes along and she
shoves it away. I ask you, now (*to Tsui-hsi*), isn't
that the height of stupidity?

TSUI-HSI: Ah well, we all get what we deserve. It's
in her stars, she doesn't deserve such good fortune.

FU-SHENG (*becoming more incensed the more he looks
at the Shrimp*): You've done for your bloody self this
time. You don't think you're going to be allowed to
stay in this manor after this, do you? My God, if I
had a daughter like that who put on such airs with me
and sent a goldmine like that off with a flea in his
ear, I'd smash her, I'd wring her neck, I'd eat her alive.
(*Pointing at the Shrimp*) I'll tell you what you are: a
damned fool. (*He pronounces these English words with
great satisfaction.*)

HU SZE: What's all the fuss about, Fu-sheng?

FU-SHENG: I — (*with a smile*) My feelings got the better of me, I can't help getting riled when I think how
obstinate the silly little bitch is.

THE SHRIMP (*going to the other end of the room and
turning to Fu-sheng*): Come over here.

FU-SHENG: What's up now? (*Glancing at Hu Sze
with a knowing wink, then swaggering across to her*)
What did you say?

THE SHRIMP (*coldly*): You got me out of the hotel by
a trick the other day.

FU-SHENG: So what?

THE SHRIMP: And now Black San is keeping his eye
on me all the time so I shall never be able to go back
for the rest of my life.

FU-SHENG: But Miss Chên at the hotel hasn't asked
for you back.

THE SHRIMP (*trembling from head to foot*): After all
the trouble I had escaping you had to go and throw me
back into Black San's hands.

FU-SHENG: You ungrateful little cuss, after us bringing you here to find you a man. You ought to be
thankful!

TSUI-HSI (*to the Shrimp*): Have you gone off your head
again?

THE SHRIMP (*ignoring her*): I — I *hate* you.

HU SZE (*going across to the Shrimp and teasing her*):
Now don't start hating people. You'd be better employed doing a bit of loving!
(*He again takes her by the hand and tries to sit her
on his lap.*)

THE SHRIMP (*flinging off Hu Sze's hands and rushing
at Fu-sheng*): I'll —
(*She slaps his face twice in succession and struggles
desperately with him.*)

FU-SHENG: The little bitch! (*He tries to fend her off.*)

TSUI-HSI (*dragging her away*): You're out of your mind.
(*Shun-tze comes in.*)

SHUN-TZE: What's up?
(*As he pushes open the door and comes in, Black San
appears in the doorway wearing a fur jacket inside out,
his face bewhiskered and his eyes savage.*)

TSUI-HSI (*to the Shrimp*): Here's Black San!

THE SHRIMP (*immediately dropping her hands and
seemingly paralysed, like a mouse that sees a cat*): Oh!

BLACK SAN (*smiling mirthlessly and beckoning the
Shrimp with a great show of politeness*): Come here.
(*The Shrimp looks from one face to another, all round
the room, but does not dare go over to Black San.*)
(*There is a moment's silence.*)

FU-SHENG: Go on, girl! (*He gives her a shove.*)

BLACK SAN (*even more amiably*): Won't you come
here?
(*The Shrimp goes slowly over.*)

BLACK SAN (*seizing her by the hand and turning to Hu
Sze*): I'm sorry about the disturbance, Mr. Hu. She
hasn't quite learnt how to behave yet. (*To Tsui-hsi*)

You look after Mr. Hu, then, Tsui-hsi. Do your best
for the gentleman and make him comfortable. Sorry,
Fu-sheng, old man, treating you like this.
(*Like a wolf with a chicken in his jaws Black San
drags the Shrimp out of the room. As the door closes
behind them we hear:*)

BLACK SAN'S VOICE (*viciously*): Take that! (*He slaps
the Shrimp's face*) And that! (*He slaps her again.*)
(*We hear the Shrimp's sharp intake of breath and the
cry of pain that follows each blow from his coarse,
heavy hand.*)
(*A pause.*)

BLACK SAN'S VOICE (*to the Shrimp*): Now get in that
room! Go on, in!
(*It seems that the Shrimp is going with him, crying
yet hardly daring to cry.*)

TSUI-HSI: What can you make of that? I've never
known such a queer child. She didn't do you any
damage, did she, Mr. Wang? I'm ever so sorry about
this.

FU-SHENG: Oh, that's all right, don't worry about that.

SHUN-TZE (*smiling*): After all, she's only a child. You
have to make allowances for children.

HU SZE: You mind your own business. Who asked
for your opinion?

SHUN-TZE: Sorry. Nobody. Let's forget I said it,
then.
(*He goes out, flustered.*)

HU SZE: How are you feeling, Fu-sheng? Did those
two slaps hurt?

FU-SHENG: Oh, I'm all right! If she can box Mr. Chin's
ears for him a couple of times, I can't very well com-
plain when she gives *me* a couple of slaps, can I?
(*The small bell outside rings.*)

A VOICE OUTSIDE: Clear a room! Visitors!

HU SZE: That's just life. If you don't enjoy yourself
when you can, you're a bloody fool. What's a couple
of slaps more or less?

FU-SHENG: Let's be going now, Mr. Hu. I think you
ought to be getting back to the hotel.

TSUI-HSI: Not on your life! (*To Fu-sheng*) You go,
if you're in such a tearing hurry! Go on!

FU-SHENG: Well, I know when I'm not wanted. I can
take a hint when I've had my face slapped.

TSUI-HSI: Now, Mr. Wang, it's not easy for any of us
in this job. You have to make allowances sometimes.
(*Shun-tze comes into the room.*)

SHUN-TZE: I'm afraid we'll have to fit you in here,
sir. I'll pull the curtain across.
(*Shun-tze moves the things on the square table on the
left across to the right and draws the curtain across
the middle of the room, thus dividing it into two halves.
He goes to the door on the left and opens it to admit
Fang Ta-sheng. Ta-sheng is wearing an unlined gown
of a deepish blue over a wadded gown. He comes in
wearily.*)

SHUN-TZE (*to Ta-sheng*): Please make yourself comfortable here, sir.

TA-SHENG: Yes.

SHUN-TZE: If you have a regular girl just tell me her
name.
(*Ta-sheng looks all round. Overcome by the odour
of the place, he covers his nose with a handkerchief.
He shakes his head.*)

SHUN-TZE: Just tell me, sir, if there's a regular girl
you have.

TA-SHENG: No, there's not. (*He coughs.*)

SHUN-TZE: A bit chilly in here, sir.
(*Meanwhile in the right-hand half of the room Hu
Sze draws Tsui-hsi to one side.*)

HU SZE: Here, I want to have a word with you.

TSUI-HSI (*smiling*): What about?

HU-SZE (*taking her by the hand*): Come over here. (*He whispers to her.*)

TSUI-HSI (*tittering*): Get away!

HU SZE: You mean that? (*He whispers again.*)

TSUI-HSI (*she gives Hu Sze a pinch and he yelps*): That'll teach you to be greedy!

HU SZE (*winking at her*): I am, too! (*He whispers again.*)

TSUI-HSI (*pretending to be angry*): The very idea! If you want to get "high" you'd better try an airship.

HU SZE: What do you mean?

TSUI-HSI: Make you think you're in heaven!
*(Hu Sze roars with laughter and pinches Tsui-hsi so that she cries out, then the two of them laugh together. Meanwhile Fu-sheng's attention has been turning more and more to the visitor in the left half of the room.)
(On the other side of the dividing curtain the action is continuing simultaneously. Ta-sheng stands there woodenly, looking extremely uncomfortable. Finally —)*

SHUN-TZE: I'll call them out so that you can see them.

TA-SHENG: I've been round a lot of places.

SHUN-TZE (*casually*): Oh, I see, you're just going for a stroll around to while away the time, eh, sir?

TA-SHENG (*as if to himself*): I still haven't found her.

SHUN-TZE: Oh, you're —

TA-SHENG: I'm looking for someone.

SHUN-TZE (*puzzled*): Loo - loo - looking for someone?

TA-SHENG: Yes, a girl who's just recently come to this district.

SHUN-TZE: Well, there's hundreds of girls round here. . . . What's her name?

TA-SHENG (*embarrassed*): She — her name's — er — she, er, she hasn't got a name.

SHUN-TZE: That makes it difficult. How old is she?

TA-SHENG: Fifteen or sixteen.

SHUN-TZE: Well, there's several that age. I'll call some of them out for you to see.

(Meanwhile, in the other half of the room —)

FU-SHENG (*stealthily pulling aside one end of the curtain and peeping through the gap into the left-hand half, suddenly, in an undertone*): Mr. Hu! Mr. Hu! Here's — here's Mr. Fang turned up.

HU SZE: Who?

FU-SHENG: Mr. Fang.

HU SZE: What? (*Hurrying across and peeping through*) Well, if it isn't, too! Who'd have thought to see him in a place like this!

(Fu-sheng suddenly dashes out of the front door on the right. Hu Sze stands by the curtain peeping through, then Tsui-hsi comes over to him, apparently asking him who it is and so on, but he just smiles and waves a hand at her, waiting inquisitively for the people in the other half of the room to say something. When she sees that she will get nothing out of him, Tsui-hsi goes disconsolately across to the dressing-table and lights a cigarette, then walks over to the front door and leans idly against the door-post.)

(On the left, Black San's voice is heard outside calling "Shun-tze! Shun-tze!")

SHUN-TZE: Coming! (*To Ta-sheng*) I'll go and fetch them for you, sir.

TA-SHENG: All right.   (*Wearily he sits down by the table.*)

(After a moment Shun-tze returns.)

SHUN-TZE: The girl you're looking for probably isn't here, sir.

TA-SHENG: How can you say that when I haven't seen anybody yet?

SHUN-TZE: Otherwise I can call out a few of about that age, if you like.

TA-SHENG: Go on, then.

(Shun-tze goes out again.)

(A pause.)

(Meanwhile, in the other half of the room, the voice of a beggar comes from outside the front door singing shulaipao *to the accompaniment of the shoulder-blade of an ox with small bells attached.)*

THE BEGGAR *(shaking the shoulder-blade, di-di-da, di-di-da, di-di-da-di-da-di-da)*:

> "Oh, here I come a jingle-jangle-jingling with my bells.
> The boss stands at the gateway touting for his gals.
> And very nice it is when trade begins to boom:
> Is this a new customer? Good! Clear a room!
> There's Tsui-hsi and Chin-kuei and also Pao-lan,
> And each of them as lovely as the famous Tiao Chan.
> Take one to bed or just sit and jaw,
> In bed it'll cost you a dollar more!"

THE BEGGAR *(resuming his feeble speaking voice)*: Wealthy sirs, and ladies, spare a copper, help me to get the price of a bed.

TSUI-HSI *(standing in the doorway)*: You again? Making a nuisance of yourself.

THE BEGGAR: Have a heart, lady. Do a fellow a good turn and you'll find you'll be out of this tomorrow, and having a bonny baby.

TSUI-HSI: Oh yeah? And you'll freeze to death tonight, you nancy-boy's whelp.

(On the left, Black San comes in.)

BLACK SAN: Here you are, sir! Here's two for you to look at.

(He lifts aside the curtain over the door.)

(Ta-sheng gets up and looks out.)

BLACK SAN: Is it one of these?

TA-SHENG *(after glancing at them)*: No, neither of them's her. She's not very old, this girl. Round face, big eyes, very blunt in the way she speaks.

BLACK SAN: Oh, you mean the one who came just the other day?

TA-SHENG: Yes, only a few days ago: let me see, yes, about four or five days ago, I think.

BLACK SAN: About this high, thin, round face, big flat feet, little round eyes, bobbed hair?

TA-SHENG: Yes, that's her.

BLACK SAN: I'll go and fetch her for you if you'll just wait a minute. (*He goes out.*)

(*Meanwhile, on the other side of the curtain:*)

THE BEGGAR (*striking his ox-bone, di-di-da, di-di-da, di-di-da-di-da-di-da*):

> "I come with my bells, as jolly as can be;
> A maiden fair before me I do see.
> With her long black plait and her curly head,
> Her pointed chin and her lips so red,
> She'll have you on your knees without a word said."

(*Di-di-da, di-di-da, di-di-da-di-da-di-da*)

> "I come with my bells all a-tinkling away,
> My lady is dressed all in silk today,
> Lovely to see and in rich array.
> Without a word she smiles so gay,
> They'll come back to see you day after day!"

THE BEGGAR: Spare a copper, lady!

TSUI-HSI (*unrelenting*): It's no use, you'll get nothing from me!

THE BEGGAR (*teasing her*): In that case I'll go on singing.

TSUI-HSI: Carry on. Who's stopping you?

(*The beggar strikes his ox-bone, di-di-da, di-di-da, di-di-da-di-da-di-da.*)

(*Meanwhile in the other half of the room the door opens and a paper-boy comes in. Unlined trousers, a tattered wadded jacket, a bearded face. Deftly he extracts a newspaper and puts it on the desk. He makes signs to indicate that he wants the money for it; he salutes, stands to attention, bows, makes inarticulate noises.*)

TA-SHENG: I've no change.

THE DUMB MAN (*holding out his hand for the money*):
Ah. . . . Ah. . . .

(*Ta-sheng gives him a ten-cent note but won't take
the change. The dumb man again bows and salutes,
then goes out, overcome with gratitude.*)

TA-SHENG (*he picks up the paper, reads a moment,
then throws it down on the table, leaning back in his
chair and gazing at the ceiling. He sighs, depressed.*):
Ah!

(*Meanwhile in the right-hand part of the room:*)

HU SZE (*letting the curtain fall, to himself*): Mad! (*He
goes to the door.*)

(*The beggar is still beating out the same di-di-da, di-
di-da, di-di-da-di-da-di-da on his ox-bone. He sings:*

> "I've sung her praises till my throat is hoarse,
> But Madam still won't open her purse.
> Don't think beggary is something low:
> It's none of your "nine lower trades," you know!
> From the families of generals and priests we came,
> And we beg from those with a sage's name.
> We've made our speeches, read poetry,
> We know the Five Bonds and the Duties Three.
> We know how to read, we can handle a brush,
> And the Five Constant Virtues are all known to us.")

THE BEGGAR: What about it, lady? Aren't you going
to spare us a copper?

TSUI-HSI: When it's as cold as this, and times as hard
as they are, I wouldn't give you money if I had it!
(*The beggar quickly improvises a reply:*

> "Times are hard, you say? Quite right,
> But yours and mine is a different plight.
> The trouble with you is that trade is slack,
> But I haven't got the price of a snack.

If I had two hundred cash or so
I wouldn't be telling you a tale of woe."

Di-di-da, di-di-da, di-di-da-di-da-di-da.)

THE BEGGAR: Now —

HU SZE: Go on, clear off! (*Throwing him a copper*)
Don't keep coming round here making a nuisance of
yourself.

THE BEGGAR: Much obliged, sir. (*The sound of foot-*
steps, then he begins banging at his ox-bone and sing-
ing next door.)
(*Fu-sheng comes in.*)

HU SZE (*pointing towards the left*): What's happening
now?

FU-SHENG (*with a crafty smile*): Have a look. (*They*
both go to the curtain and peep through.)
(*On the other side, Black San and Shun-tze come in.*)

BLACK SAN: Here you are, sir, this must be your girl-
friend.

TA-SHENG (*going to the doorway and looking but greatly*
disappointed): No, it isn't, that's not her.

SHUN-TZE: But we can't help you if you don't give
us a name.

TA-SHENG (*suddenly*): Have you got one here called
the Shrimp?

SHUN-TZE: The Shrimp?

TA-SHENG: That's right.

SHUN-TZE: No.

BLACK SAN (*with a crafty smile*): That's a rum name.

TA-SHENG (*picking up his hat*): Sorry to have troubled
you. (*With his head bent, he is about to go out of the*
room.)
(*Black San bars his way, holding out his hand.*)

TA-SHENG: What's this for?

BLACK SAN: Don't we get anything, after all the running about we've been doing for you?

TA-SHENG (*staring in surprise*): You charge even for that?

BLACK SAN: What sort of a place do you think this is? Do you think we live on air?

TA-SHENG (*with a pitying smile at Black San's desperate expression, taking out some money*): Here, take this.

SHUN-TZE (*hurriedly stretching out his hand*): Thank you.

BLACK SAN (*knocking Shun-tze's hand aside*): You're joking! You're not throwing coppers to a beggar, you know.

(*In the side-room to the left the baby begins to cry. Tsui-hsi pulls aside the dividing curtain across the centre and goes to the left-hand side of the room. Seeing Ta-sheng she stops and stares at him. Ta-sheng turns his head away in distaste and begins coughing, then, covering his nose with one hand and throwing some money on the table with the other, he immediately hurries out.*)

(*Puzzled, Tsui-hsi goes into the little side-room on the left and again begins soothing the baby to sleep.*)

(*Black San breaks into coarse laughter.*)

(*Shun-tze draws the centre curtain right back.*)

BLACK SAN: If you'll make yourself at home for a minute, Mr. Hu, I'll fetch Little Tsui to look after you.

FU-SHENG: Don't bother, Black San. We'll have to be going now.

HU SZE: We've been here quite a time.

BLACK SAN: Now don't go rushing off before you've had a chance to enjoy yourself. (*He hurries out shouting "Little Tsui!"*)

FU-SHENG: We'd better hurry back. You ought to show off your new outfit to Mrs. Ku.

HU SZE (*remembering his nickname of "the most handsome boy in China," brightening up*): By the way, don't you think this outfit looks well on me?

FU-SHENG: I do indeed! I think it's the best I've ever seen you in.

HU SZE (*unconsciously beginning to posture and preen himself again, dusting his clothes, self-satisfied*): It's not bad, I don't think.

(*Black San comes in, followed by the Shrimp.*)

BLACK SAN: Now come and look after Mr. Hu properly. Then perhaps Mr. Hu will take kindly to you. Say how d'you do to Mr. Hu.

THE SHRIMP (*sobbing out the words*): How — how — how d'you do, Mr. Hu?

BLACK SAN: Apologize to Mr. Wang.

(*The Shrimp just stands there looking at Fu-sheng.*)

BLACK SAN: Go on, say "I won't dare do it again, Mr. Wang."

THE SHRIMP (*sobbing out each syllable*): I — I — I — won't dare do it again. Mr. — Mr. — Mr. Wang.

FU-SHENG: That's quite all right.

BLACK SAN (*very pleased with himself*): Now pour Mr. Hu a cup of tea and ask Mr. Wang if he'll come again tomorrow with Mr. Hu.

HU SZE: All right, tomorrow, then. (*Getting up*) Now let's forget it and drop the formalities. Now everything's all right.

(*Tsui-hsi comes out of the side-room.*)

TSUI-HSI: What's all this talk about going? I won't let either of you go. What was it you were saying just now, Mr. Hu?

(*She whispers in his ear.*)

HU SZE (*nodding repeatedly*): Yes, that's right. (*With a wicked smile*) But I really am busy. I can't manage tonight. See you tomorrow.

FU-SHENG (*smiling*): Yes, we are busy. We'll see you tomorrow.

BLACK SAN: This time she found herself with Mr. Hu, who's a very reasonable sort. Now, what happens if

she rubs a difficult customer up the wrong way?   We'd
be out of business before we knew where we were!

TSUI-HSI (*holding on to Hu Sze*):   Promise you'll come
tomorrow, then?

(*Hu Sze nods, smiling insincerely.*) ·

(*By now the Shrimp has poured the tea and is taking
it across to Hu Sze*).

FU-SHENG (*teasing her*):   Careful now, don't scald your
hand, Miss.   .

(*The Shrimp goes up to Hu Sze with drooping head and
tear-filled eyes.*)

FU-SHENG: See that, Mr. Hu?   Little Tsui's making
eyes at you.

(*The Shrimp throws an angry glance over her shoulder
at Fu-sheng.*)

HU SZE (*delighted*): Is she? (*Trying to pinch her
cheek*) So the little shrimp's fallen for me, has she?

THE SHRIMP (*she suddenly turns her head, not expecting to find Hu Sze so close to her.   The cup collides with
Hu Sze's hand and the tea splashes on his clothes*): Oh!

HU SZE: Look at that!

BLACK SAN (*bellowing*):   What the hell do you think
you're doing!

THE SHRIMP (*losing her nerve with fright she lets her
hand slip and the whole cup of tea is spilt over Hu Sze's
new clothes*):   Oh!

HU SZE (*his face dark with rage*):   Blast you!   You
bloody little idiot, you!   (*He hurriedly mops himself
with a handkerchief*).

BLACK SAN (*springing across to where the Shrimp is
standing, his hand raised to strike her*):   You bloody
little — (*The Shrimp takes refuge behind Tsui-hsi.*)

TSUI-HSI (*restraining Black San*):   Don't hit her now!

FU-SHENG (*also restraining Black San*):   Hold it, Black
San, the clothes come first.

BLACK SAN (*in a flurry*):   Quick, get a cloth, Shun-tze.
(*Shun-tze dashes in with a cloth.   Everyone is mop-*

*ping at the clothes together except for the Shrimp, who
stands rooted to the spot with fright.)*

HU SZE (*infuriated*):   Get away! Get away! Don't wipe
at them like that! (*He goes and looks at his clothes
under the light.*) Look at that, a whole outfit practically
ruined.   My God — (*To Fu-sheng*) Come on, we're
getting out of this! (*Suddenly striding across to the
Shrimp*)   You guttersnipe, I'll — (*He makes as if to
attack her, but the Shrimp backs away and he swings
round away from her.*) Baggage! (*Suddenly taking
out a wad of banknotes from his pocket and turning
back to the Shrimp*)   See this?   I'm not short of money.
But for a stupid little idiot like you (*turning to Black
San*) I wouldn't give a penny! (*Turning to Shun-tze*)
Give this to Tsui-hsi for looking after us. (*He gives
him a banknote.*)   And this is for the people outside.
(*He gives him another note.*)

SHUN-TZE: Thank you.

HU SZE (*with a nod*):   Come on. (*To Fu-sheng*) Let's
get back to the hotel.   (*He stalks out.*)
(*Fu-sheng and Shun-tze follow him out.*)

TSUI-HSI (*seeing them out*):   Come again tomorrow, Mr.
Hu!   Don't forget! (*She comes quickly back into the
room.*)

BLACK SAN (*glaring at the Shrimp like a wild beast, his
voice low*):   Come here.   We're going in there. (*He
indicates the little side-room on the left.*)
(*The Shrimp takes a few steps, then her legs fail her
and she collapses with a thump on to her knees.*)

BLACK SAN (*going across to the Shrimp and pulling her
by the arm*):   Come on!

TSUI-HSI (*putting her arms round the Shrimp*):   Don't
hit her, Black San! (*Imploring*) It wasn't her fault,
you mustn't hit her!

BLACK SAN (*pulling out a whip from under the table*):
You keep out of this!

TSUI-HSI: Black San, she couldn't stand another thrashing.
BLACK SAN (*pushing her over*):   Get the bloody hell
out of it, you!
(*Tsui-hsi gives a cry of pain, then begins rubbing her
injured hand.*)
BLACK SAN: Come on!
(*He drags the Shrimp into the next room and fastens
the door.*)
TSUI-HSI (*suddenly remembering her baby, she rushes
across to the little door on the left and bangs on it*):
Open the door, Black San, my baby's in there.   Open
the door, open the door!
(*There is no reply from Black San, who is busy curs-
· ing at the Shrimp and plying the whip on her; she
seems to be gritting her teeth and steeling herself
against each lash of the whip.*)
TSUI-HSI (*hammering at the door, panic-stricken*): Open
the door, open the door!   You'll frighten my baby.   My
baby!
(*The child begins to cry.*)
TSUI-HSI (*shouting desperately*):   Open the door, open
the door!   Black San!   Don't be frightened, my precious, Mummy's coming!
(*Unable to bear the pain, the Shrimp begins to howl,
and this combined with the crying of the baby attracts
a number of curious onlookers outside.   Shun-tze hurries in.*)
TSUI-HSI (*frantically*):   Open the door!   (*She beats on
it wildly*)   Open the door!   Black San!   If you don't
open up I'll call the police.
SHUN-TZE: Black San, there's somebody outside to see
you.
(*Black San opens the door and comes out carrying the
whip, his face damp with sweat.*)
BLACK SAN (*over his shoulder*):   I'm letting you off
light this time, you little bitch.

(*Tsui-hsi immediately runs into the room, where the crying of the baby and the Shrimp's sobbing can be heard.*)

BLACK SAN (*to Shun-tze*): Who is it? Who wants me?

SHUN-TZE: Somebody from the hotel.

(*The little bell outside rings.*)

(*A pause.*)

BLACK SAN: What's it about?

SHUN-TZE: He says Mr. Chin wants to see you about something.

ANOTHER VOICE: Visitor staying the night! Outside, anybody not fixed up for the night!

BLACK SAN: Let's go and see him, then. (*Towards the small door on the left*) Come on out! Outside!

(*The Shrimp drags herself painfully out.*)

BLACK SAN (*pointing with the whip*): I'm letting you off this time. There's somebody staying the night. Go out and see them. By God, if you don't get a customer again tonight you needn't come and see me tomorrow morning. D'you hear?

THE SHRIMP (*sobbing*): Yes.

BLACK SAN: Now go. Wipe your eyes and go and see the visitors.

(*The Shrimp goes out with bowed head.*)

BLACK SAN: I'm going now, Shun-tze. See you in the morning.

SHUN-TZE: Right you are. See you tomorrow.

(*Black San goes out.*)

SHUN-TZE: Here, Tsui-hsi, come out here. The cripple's fed up with waiting. You'd better hurry up and go out to him.

(*Tsui-hsi appears through the small doorway on the left.*)

TSUI-HSI: Whew! What a life!

(*Tsui-hsi and Shun-tze go out together, leaving the room empty.*)

THE VOICE OF AN ATTENDANT OUTSIDE: Lights
going out! Lights going out!

THE VOICE OF A HAWKER (*bleakly*): Shortbread!
Shortbread!

(*The tock-tock-tocking of a watchman's hollow wooden
gong goes by.*)

ANOTHER ATTENDANT'S VOICE (*calling out the girls'
names in a low voice since the visitors have now gone
to bed*): Precious Orchid, Turquoise Jade, Cherry-
apple, Little Tsui.

(*Shun-tze comes in and switches off the light, then
takes a candle from a drawer and lights it. It is now
dark in the room.*)

(*Just as Shun-tze is going out, the Shrimp comes slowly
in.*)

(*Next door and across the courtyard men and women
are laughing and conversing with subdued voices.*)

SHUN-TZE: Well, did you get him?

THE SHRIMP (*shaking her head*): No.

SHUN-TZE: How's that?

THE SHRIMP (*with a sob*): He said I was too young.

SHUN-TZE (*sighing*): You'd better be off to bed on your
own, then.

THE SHRIMP: Yes.

SHUN-TZE (*consoling her*): D—don't worry. Tomorrow can take care of itself; d—d—don't think about
it.

(*In the distance Tsui-hsi is weeping and shouting.*)

A MAN'S VOICE: Will you come home or won't you?
Eh?

TSUI-HSI'S VOICE: Go on, hit me, then! Hit me! If
you don't kill me today you're none of your father's
getting.

THE SHRIMP (*standing up*): Who's that?

SHUN-TZE: Tsui-hsi. Her hu—hu—sband's laying into
her. (*Looking out of the window*) Poor bitch. Not
much of a life she's had. Her husband got the pox

after he married her and now he's a cripple. Two babies b—b—blind from birth. Then there's his old lady, paralysed and bedridden. And the whole family scrapes along on wha—what they can get out of this place.

THE SHRIMP (*sitting down again, staring absently in front of her*): Yes, mm, yes.

SHUN-TZE: Here she is. (*Shouting out of the door*) Tsui-hsi.

(*Tsui-hsi comes in tearful and sobbing.*)

SHUN-TZE: What happened?

TSUI-HSI (*to herself*): By God, I will go home with you! This very night I will! And when I get home we'll separate. There's no sense in going on like this. (*Muttering, she goes into the room on the left.*)

SHUN-TZE (*watching her in*): Tut.

(*Tsui-hsi comes out again with the baby in her arms.*)

THE SHRIMP: Is he asleep?

TSUI-HSI (*choked with sobs*): Yes, Little Tsui, he . . . he . . . is. (*With a sob between each word*) That . . . that . . . all-nighter . . . just now, did . . . did you . . . get him?

(*The Shrimp hangs her head but doesn't reply.*)

SHUN-TZE (*shaking his head*): No, she didn't.

TSUI-HSI: How . . . how was that?

SHUN-TZE: The usual. Thought she was too young.

TSUI-HSI (*stroking the Shrimp's face*): You . . . you poor kid. Still, never mind, you can have my bed all to yourself tonight. You won't have me taking up half of it. It gets cold at night, so have plenty of covers on. Don't . . . don't freeze. Don't start worrying about tomorrow till it comes. Look after yourself while you can, because if you fall ill in this place no . . . nobody will give a damn.

(*The Shrimp looks at her, then overcome, she flings her arms round Tsui-hsi and bursts into tears.*)

TSUI-HSI (*shedding tears of anguish and drawing her to her*): Little Tsui, Little Tsui, don't . . . don't cry. I'm . . . going now. First thing . . . tomorrow morning I'll . . . I'll come and see you.
(*The Shrimp sobs.*)
TSUI-HSI: I'll . . . I'll be off, then.
THE SHRIMP: Yes.
SHUN-TZE: Well, I'm off to bed. (*To the Shrimp*) You'd better get to bed yourself.
THE SHRIMP: All right.
(*Tsui-hsi and Shun-tze go out together.*)
A VOICE OUTSIDE: Lights going out! Lights going out!
(*The watchman's wooden gong. The stage becomes even darker.*)
THE HAWKER'S VOICE (*bleakly*): Shortbread! Shortbread!
(*The Shrimp suddenly stands up and goes silently into the side-room on the left.*)
(*The stage is now empty.*)
(*The sound of laughter from a couple in a room across the courtyard.*)
THE WOMAN'S VOICE: Go on, get away with you. What do you have to come twenty miles to see me for, when you've got plenty of girls back home?
THE MAN'S VOICE (*muffled*): . . . I
THE WOMAN'S VOICE: Stop it, don't do that! (*Giggling*) Aren't you shy, this being your first time?
THE MAN'S VOICE (*still muffled*): . . . Mm. . . .
(*The Shrimp reappears from the side-room trailing her slippered feet, a hempen rope in her hand. She stands by the table with wide staring eyes as if seeing a vision, nodding her head. As if in a trance she goes to each of the front doors in turn, closes them, and locks them. She begins to tremble, then summons up her courage and goes to the small door on the left, where she stops. She moves a chair over, stands on it, and ties the rope*)

to the lintel of the door in the form of a small noose.
Then she gets down again. She paces abstractedly up
and down, then suddenly stops.)

THE SHRIMP (*in a low, choking voice*): Oh, Father!
(*She kneels facing the noose and kowtows three times,*
then stands up. With a sigh she climbs up on the chair,
puts her head through the noose, and kicks the chair
away. . . . Such a tiny, such a weak, pathetic little
life now hangs from the lintel.)

THE HAWKER'S VOICE (*desolately*): Shortbread!
Shortbread!
(*Meanwhile, apart from the sound of the watchman's*
wooden gong, there also comes from outside:)

A MAN'S VOICE (*singing suggestively*):

> "*You called me your little sweetheart,*
> *sleepless until the dawn.*
> *When morning came,*
> *you left my bed.*

> "*Lover,*
> *I can't bear to lose you;*
> *one night together,*
> *and I love you for ever more.*"

(*The sound of a woman weeping softly, as if at a great*
distance.)
(*As the Shrimp hangs there, the flickering light of the*
candle dances on her feet. One of her backless slip-
pers drops quietly to the floor, and there is now no one
in the room.)
(*The stage gradually blacks out.*)

— *THE CURTAIN FALLS* —

ALTERNATIVE ENDING TO THIS ACT

It may be thought that the end of this act is too harrowing, so, for the purpose of stage presentation, I have changed it to the following:

(from the 30th line of p. 135 to the end of the act)

(The Shrimp reappears from the side-room trailing her slippered feet, a hempen rope in her hand. She stands by the table with wide staring eyes as if seeing a vision, nodding her head. As if in a trance she goes to each of the front doors in turn, closes them, and locks them. She trembles all over, restraining her tears, then with an expression of alarm she goes to the side-door on the left and stops.)

THE HAWKER'S VOICE *(desolately)*: Shortbread! Shortbread!

(The sound of a watchman's wooden gong in the distance.)

(She moves a chair over to the door, stands on it, and ties the rope to the lintel of the door in the form of a small noose. She steels herself for the deed . . . but with a shiver of terror she gets down again and stands there in a daze.)

A MAN'S VOICE *(singing softly and suggestively)*:

"You called me your little sweetheart,
sleepless until the dawn.
When morning came,
you left my bed.

"Lover,
I can't bear to lose you;
one night together,
and I love you for ever more."

(The sound of a woman weeping softly, as if at a great distance.)

(*Undecided, the Shrimp takes a few unsteady steps in time with the woman's weeping, then, unable to bear her inaction any longer, she suddenly flings herself face downward on the floor and weeps broken-heartedly.*)

THE HAWKER'S VOICE (*desolately*): Shortbread! Shortbread!

(*The sound of a watchman's wooden gong far away in the distance.*)

(*The stage gradually blacks out.*)

— *THE CURTAIN FALLS* —

Act IV

(*The same night as Act III, at about four o'clock in the morning. We are back in the luxuriously-furnished sitting-room of a suite in the X Hotel.*

The curtains in the room are drawn, and in the harsh glare of the light the bizarre furniture and furnishings of the room jar on the eyes until one feels dazed by it all. The air is thick with cigarette-smoke and a vile reek of scent and cosmetics. Bottles are strewn higgledy-piggledy on the floor and the liquids from them, precious as gold, is soaking unheeded into the carpet, staining the plush of the armchairs yellow and flooding the marble top of the small tea-table. In the centre, by the legs of a small armchair, are the fragments of a broken champagne-glass. The shiny clock on the wall points to four o'clock.

The hubbub of a game of mahjong still comes from the room on the left, with now a period of quiet broken only by the occasional crisp click of a mahjong tile, now a period of talk and joking, curses and exclamations, slaps of annoyance on the mahjong table, and derisive laughter . . . all mingled with the sound of the tiles being shuffled round on the surface of the table.

When the curtain rises, Pai-lu is standing alone by the window, her back to the audience, holding the curtains aside and looking out. She is wearing a black velours dress edged with a patterned orange border shot with black dots. The fact that she is all in black gives her an appearance of severity.

She stands alone by the window, and there is not a sound from anything in the room.

A pause.

139

*The door on the left opens wide and immediately a
torrent of laughter and noise from the mahjong players
bursts into the room.)*

VOICES FROM THE NEXT ROOM: Lulu! Lulu!
*(Pai-lu pays no attention to them, but stands there
motionless.)*
GEORGY'S VOICE: Lulu! Lulu!
GEORGY *(to the people in the next room as he emerges)*:
No, no, I'll be straight back. *(Self-confidently)* See if
I can't persuade her.
*(Georgy now emerges. He is wearing an impeccable
European-style suit with his tie adrift and his waistcoat
buttons undone. In one hand he grasps a champagne-
bottle, in the other a glass. He goes over towards Pai-
lu in boisterous high spirits.)*
GEORGY *(going unsteadily and erratically across to Pai-
lu, the spirit suddenly moving him)*: Ah! My little
Lulu! *(Looking her up and down and gesticulating, as
if declaiming a poem) Si belle! Si charmante! et si
mélancolique!*
(Pai-lu remains gazing out of the window, motionless.)
GEORGY *(going up to her)*: You are beautiful! You
really are beautiful this evening! *(Carried away, his
eyes closed in rapturous appreciation)* Beautiful!
Absolutely beautiful! You really do know how to dress,
so melancholically, so bewitchingly! *And* you know
how to wear perfume, it smells so — *(sniffing and
making a long-drawn-out "Mm!")* — so delicate, yet so
mysteriously distant! Ah! The moment I smell the
fragrance of your perfume —*ah non,* the pure fragrance
that emanates from your beautiful body, it takes me
back to when I first went to Paris. . . . *(Floating
away on the mists of memory)* Ah, those Paris nights!
Paris at night! *(With admiration)* Mm! *Exquise!*
PAI-LU *(still not looking round)*: You're drunk again,
I suppose.

GEORGY: Drunk? I feel absolutely on top of the world tonight! Did you see Miss Liu a short while ago? She says she wants to marry me, she insists on marrying me, but I told her — (*haughtily*) I said: "You? (*Contemptuously*) You marry me? You stand there and tell me you want to marry me? You?" (*With a gesture of dismissal*) "The only person in this world who's worthy of George Chang is Chen Pai-lu!" (*He expects Pai-lu to laugh, but she doesn't*) Why, Lulu, why don't you laugh?

PAI-LU (*her manner unchanged*): What is there to laugh at in that? (*In an undertone*) Anything left in that bottle?

GEORGY (*surprised*): You want another drink?

PAI-LU: Yes.

GEORGY: See how I dance attendance on you? Everything you need to hand. (*While he is pouring her a drink, Mrs. Ku's voice comes from the room on the right, calling Pai-lu's name. When he has poured it he hands it to Pai-lu.*)
(*Pai-lu swallows it down at one gulp and hands the glass back to him without even glancing at it.*)
(*Mrs. Ku comes out of the room on the right. She is dressed and bejewelled as brightly and dazzlingly as ever. She enters in a froth of agitation.*)

KU (*in the doorway*): Where are your sleeping-tablets, Pai-lu? (*Suddenly noticing Georgy*) Oh! Doctor Chang. So it was you two coming in here on the sly and talking, was it?

PAI-LU: In the little cupboard beside my bed.

GEORGY: What's the trouble, then, Mrs. Ku?

KU (*rubbing her heart*): My heart pains me. I'm suffering.

GEORGY: What's the cause of it this time?

KU: It's that unfeeling creature been upsetting me again. An upset like this will lose me three nights' sleep. I really must take some sleeping-pills home with

me to take. But that's enough about my troubles: you
two carry on with your conversation. (*She turns to go
back through the door.*)

GEORGY: Here, don't go. Come and sit in here with us
for a while and have a chat.

KU: No, no, impossible. I'm in agony with this heart
of mine. I must go and take some of Doctor Ledoux's
medicine.

GEORGY: Yes, but look, you can take it in here just
the same, can't you?

KU: Just listen to my heart, though. It is pounding
away again. (*Clasping her heart with both hands and
grimacing as if in agony*) Ooh! I must go and lie down
for a while.

(*Suddenly the door on the left opens wide and a hubbub of noise and laughter is again unleashed into the
room.*)

(*Mrs. Ku goes out left.*)

MISS LIU'S VOICE: Georgy!

GEORGY (*laying a finger across his lips as a sign to Miss
Liu who is through the doorway on the left*): Shh!
(*He motions towards Pai-lu and makes signs to Miss
Liu to come in.*)

MISS LIU'S VOICE (*severely*): Georgy!

GEORGY (*signalling to her not to shout, his finger still
on his lips*): Shh!

MISS LIU'S VOICE (*even more severely*): Are you
coming or aren't you?

GEORGY: I'm coming! I'm coming! Right away!
(*Smiling nervously, he goes through the door on the
left.*)

(*A pause.*)

PAI-LU (*she slowly turns round, wearing a dismal expression. She has been drinking too much and her
face is flushed. She raps herself lightly on the chest,
and after two or three raps she lets her hand swing
limply down as if in despair. She heaves a sigh*): U-u-

uh. (*She lifts her head. Tears are trickling down from the corners of her eyes. She spreads her handkerchief over her eyes.*)

(*A knock on the door.*)

PAI-LU (*removing the handkerchief and wiping her eyes*): Who is it?

FU-SHENG'S VOICE: It's me, Miss.

PAI-LU: Come in.

(*Fu-sheng comes in. He has been back in the hotel for some time now, so he is in uniform.*)

FU-SHENG: 'Morning, Miss.

PAI-LU: What is it?

FU-SHENG (*noticing that Pai-lu has been crying*): Oh, didn't you want me?

PAI-LU: No.

FU-SHENG: Oh, all right, very good. . . . (*Looking at Pai-lu*) You've been overdoing the drinks tonight, Miss.

PAI-LU: I know.

FU-SHENG (*looking all round*): Isn't Mr. Fang around?

PAI-LU: He isn't back yet. Why, you want to see him?

FU-SHENG: Nothing important. Another telegram came a short while ago. It's for Mr. Fang.

PAI-LU: Where is it?

FU-SHENG (*producing it from a pocket*): Do you want it?

PAI-LU: I'll give it to him myself later on.

(*Fu-sheng gives her the telegram.*)

PAI-LU: It's early yet, isn't it?

FU-SHENG: Early! It's after four!

PAI-LU (*absently*): Haven't those people gone yet?

FU-SHENG (*looking at the door on the left*): They're all eating and drinking and they've got plenty to keep them amused here, so I can't imagine them being ready to go.

PAI-LU (*nodding sadly*): So that's all they come here for: to amuse themselves.

FU-SHENG: Well, of course!

PAI-LU: And what will happen when they've had all the amusement they want?

FU-SHENG: Well, they'll go home, of course. They've all got their own homes to go to — can't stay in a hotel all your life, now can you!

PAI-LU (*in the same colourless voice*): Then why haven't they had all they want? (*In a low voice to herself*) No, one can't stay all one's life in a hotel. (*Shaking her head*) I've probably had all the amusement I want. (*Sitting down*) Yes, I've had enough of it (*pensively*), I'd like to go home myself, back to my old home.

FU-SHENG (*astonished*): But Miss, you mean you've got a home?

PAI-LU: I've had enough, I should go back home.

FU-SHENG: Are you serious about this, Miss?

PAI-LU: Yes.

FU-SHENG (*hurriedly*): Look, Miss, if you really are thinking of going back to your old home, what about all your unpaid debts here? You'll have to —

PAI-LU: Yes, I know I'm deep in debt. But surely I've paid in full, all the years I've been here?

FU-SHENG: Now look, Miss, you've just paid up eight hundred and now you're another two thousand in debt. If you go on throwing money around like that, you'll never be out of debt to the end of your days. They were here again this afternoon. Now just have a look at these bills. (*Taking them out of his pocket again*) Altogether they come to —

PAI-LU: No, don't bother to get them out. I don't want to see them.

FU-SHENG: But they say you must pay up without fail by tomorrow afternoon. I did my best to talk them round —

PAI-LU: Who asked you to try and talk them round? "Every grievance has its incurrer and every debt its debtor." I didn't go and plead with them myself, so why must you plead with them?

FU-SHENG: But, Miss —

PAI-LU (*crossly*): I know, I know. No need to say it again. Money! Money! Money! Why must you keep on harrying me with it?

(*The telephone rings.*)

FU-SHENG (*picking up the receiver*): Hullo. . . . Who's that? Oh . . . this is Suite 52, Miss Chen's.

PAI-LU: Who is it?

FU-SHENG (*covering the mouthpiece with his hand*): Mrs. Li. (*Speaking into the receiver again*) Oh, I see, yes. Mr. Li's not here. He was here this afternoon, but he went a good while ago. . . . Yes . . . yes . . . Mr. Li rang Mr. Pan here a short while ago and said would he be so kind as to wait for him as he'd be over again soon. . . . Well, why not give us another ring later on? (*He puts down the receiver.*)

PAI-LU: What was all that about?

FU-SHENG: Mr. Li's son's seriously ill and Mrs. Li wants him back home quickly.

PAI-LU: I see. All right, that'll be all, then.

(*Mr. Pan comes in through the centre door, his face beaming.*)

(*Fu-sheng ushers him into the room, then goes out through the centre door.*)

PAN: Lulu, Lulu, your visitors haven't gone, have they?

PAI-LU: No.

PAN: Excellent. Don't let any of them go. We must make this a party to end all parties.

PAI-LU: What for?

PAN: I think a real stroke of good luck has come my way at last. I've got some good news.

PAI-LU: Good news, you say? Why, has Mr. Chin agreed to give you another week to return his deposit?

PAN: No, nothing like that; Mr. Chin agreed to that a couple of days ago. Now let me tell you: Government bonds are going to rise further after all. Right up.

Higher than they've ever been. And that's going to put me on my feet again! You know I suddenly heard this morning that the news of a rise was only a rumour put about by Mr. Chin as a trick. They said he was putting a rumour round that he was buying in quite a lot himself so that everybody else would buy, whereas in actual fact he was getting rid of his own holdings and he wanted to make himself a good selling market. When I heard that I was in an absolute panic! I thought I'd fallen into his trap and that the value of my holdings was going to slump right down, so that every penny I possess and a lot more would be called for on settlement-day, thanks to him. You can well imagine why I was panicking at the thought of going bankrupt, with all my long string of businesses and all my large family, especially at my age. I tell you Lulu, I even had a revolver ready, I — (*He starts coughing.*)

PAI-LU (*unmoved*): You poor thing.

PAN (*in high spirits*): There's nothing poor about me now. I tell you, one must have money. Without money, life's not worth living. But now, Lulu, I really am rich. In a couple of days I'll have piles of money, and a few days later I may well have more, much more. (*With sudden generosity*) And from now onwards I'm going to do something for charities, get some good deeds against my name in The Book, make up for what I haven't done in the past —

PAI-LU: Yet you let Mr. Chin have the Shrimp back without a qualm. That's something that's going to take a lot of making up for.

PAN (*suddenly remembering*): Oh, what's happened to the Shrimp? You mean to say you haven't got her back yet?

PAI-LU: Got her back? She's disappeared as completely as if she'd jumped into the sea. I've hunted for her, and so has Ta-sheng, but there's not a trace of her.

PAN: Don't worry. I'm rich now, plenty of money. I can get the Shrimp back for you alive and kicking, just like that. That'll cheer you up.

PAI-LU (*hopelessly*): All right, then. Oh, by the way, did you know that Li Shih-ching is coming to see you here soon?

PAN: Yes. He tells me he's got good news for me. He's a stupid oaf, though, and thinks he can treat me as he likes and get away with it. I'm going to make him sit up and take notice this time, though.

PAI-LU: Why, what do you mean?

(*Mrs. Ku comes in from the left.*)

KU: Lulu! Lulu! — Why, Mr. Pan, where have you been all night? (*Coquettishly*) I really don't know, abandoning us here, ignoring us, you men really are the limit! — Oh, yes, I know what I was going to tell you, Mr. Pan: you should see the way Hu Sze's quietened down since he's been working for the film company. You were right, you know. One can always trust you to suggest the right thing and recommend the right person for a position, Mr. Pan. (*Before Pan can reply she slips over to the dressing-mirror on the wardrobe on the left. She looks at herself in it, then suddenly turns to Pai-lu.*) Lulu, how do I look now? Not too ghastly, do I?

PAN (*having no alternative*): If you'll be here to keep Mrs. Ku company, Lulu, I'll go in the other room to see your visitors. (*He goes out left.*)

KU: Are you leaving us, Mr. Pan? (*Unable to contain herself any longer, to Pai-lu*) Do you think he ever will come? The heartless creature, he told me to wait for him here at your place. He was going to teach me some opera — *Staying the Night and Killing Hsichiao*, it was. It's nearly morning and there's not a sign of him yet. Oh, I really — I — I really think I should tell Fu-sheng to ask him —

PAI-LU (*out of patience with her, she calls him before she has finished speaking*): Fu-sheng! Fu-sheng!
(*Fu-sheng comes in through the centre door.*)

PAI-LU: Do you know where Mr. Hu Sze has gone?

FU-SHENG: No, I don't.

KU (*ill-humouredly*): He'll never admit to knowing anything.

FU-SHENG: I assure you . . . (*With an ingratiating smile*) I really don't know. Though I seem to remember him saying that first he'd have to go and —

KU (*explosively*): Change his clothes!

FU-SHENG (*with an assumed smile, simultaneously*): Change his clothes.

KU (*annoyed and upset*): Change his clothes! Change his clothes! Is that all you can keep telling me?

PAI-LU: What? (*To Fu-sheng*) Do you know where Hu Sze has gone?

FU-SHENG (*humbly*): Mrs. Ku's asked me four or five times already, so no wonder madam is getting tired of hearing it over and over again. After all, madam does tend to get anxious about things, and for another thing—

KU: Go on, get away! Keep 'madam'-ing me like that! It makes me feel cross just to look at you. You've no right to come in here making me more ill than I am already.

FU-SHENG: Very good, as you say. (*He goes out through the centre door.*)

KU (*thumping her heart*): There, now my heart's beginning to pain me again. And on top of that Hu Sze's taking his new job less and less seriously, even though he's only been with the film company two days. It makes me wish I were dead! Lulu! I'm taking all your sleeping-pills away with me.

PAI-LU: Why, you're not going to start taking sleeping-pills, are you?

KU: Yes, I must take some.

PAI-LU: I don't think you really need to. You'd better
let me have them back. (*She holds out her hand.*)

KU: No, I absolutely must take some. If I can have a
good sleep I'll recover my temper. Dr. Ledoux says
that an hour's good sleep is as good as a square meal.
I'll *have* a square meal, too! I'll make Hu Sze sit up!

PAI-LU: Oh, I see. But I'd better warn you that these
sleeping-tablets are very strong. If you take ten you
won't be here in the morning. So you'd better be
careful.

KU (*looking at the bottle of tablets*): Well, so ten of
them can kill you?

PAI-LU: Yes, ten's enough.

KU: Well . . . in that case I'll . . . I'll just take half
a tablet.

PAI-LU: From what you were saying just now I
thought —   .

KU: Oh, I see (*suddenly understanding*), you mean you
thought I wanted to commit suicide with them? No fear
of that. I'm not daft, I want a few more years of
enjoyment yet! Hm! I'm just beginning to learn a thing
or two, I've — humph! If Hu Sze's going to leave me
one day, I may as well have done with him. I'll find
somebody else, I'll — I'll make him really angry!

PAI-LU (*looking at her dispassionately*): Aren't you
tired?

KU: Why, yes, I am a bit tired. I must have a few
games of mahjong to rest my brain. Come along in
with me.

PAI-LU: No, you go on without me. I want to sit here
on my own for a while.

(*Ku goes out left.*)

(*A knock on the centre door.*)

PAI-LU: Who is it?

(*Ta-sheng enters through the centre door.*)

PAI-LU: Just got back?

TA-SHENG: I've been back a short while. I heard Mrs. Ku in here so I didn't come in.

PAI-LU (*looking at him*): Well? Have you found the Shrimp?

TA-SHENG (*shaking his head*): No. I went round every single place of that type looking for her, but she wasn't at any of them.

PAI-LU (*losing hope*): Just as I expected. (*A pause, then she takes his arm and sits him down*) Tired?

TA-SHENG: A bit, though my mind is very much awake. I'm busy thinking. The last day or two I've been thinking hard about something. (*Suddenly*) Tell me, why must people be so cruel to one another?

PAI-LU (*smiling*): Is that what you've been thinking about?

TA-SHENG: I can't make out why you people allow a beast like this Chin to go on living.

PAI-LU: Why, you must be a simpleton. I tell you, it's not a question of whether we allow Chin to go on living: it's a question of whether he'll allow us to go on living.

TA-SHENG (*deep in thought*): It's right enough, what you say. I should have a closer look at these creatures here. Now I've seen them as they really are. Though I can't say I've done the same with you yet. I just don't understand why you have to mix with them. You must realize that they're monsters, a lot of beasts. I can see that you loathe them too, Chu-chun, yet you will go on pretending that you don't mind, deceiving yourself all the time.

PAI-LU (*bristling with sudden sarcasm*): You've great faith in your own cleverness, haven't you.

TA-SHENG: There you go again, Chu-chun. No, I'm not clever. But I've great faith in your cleverness. Now don't try to deceive me. You're unhappy. Remember we're old friends, so please don't keep on being obstinate with me. I know you've learnt to keep a stiff

upper lip and to lie like this so that people will think
you're happy, but your eyes are not steady, your eyes
can't hide your fear, your doubts, your dissatisfaction.
One may deceive others, Chu-chun, but one cannot deceive oneself. If you go on like this you'll die of
frustration.

PAI-LU (*with a sigh*): What do you think I ought to
do, then?

TA-SHENG: You must get married, Chu-chun. I'd like
to find you a husband, a *real* man. You should get
away from this place at once.

PAI-LU (*meditatively*): Get away — yes. But — get
married? (*She sighs.*) I've tried it. But (*sighing*) it was
dreary and dull, and rather ridiculous when you come
to look back on it.

TA-SHENG: Who was he?

PAI-LU: Someone rather like you.

TA-SHENG: Like me?

PAI-LU: Yes, very much so. — He was a fool.

TA-SHENG: Oh.

PAI-LU: He was a poet, you see. (*Recalling memories*)
He . . . he was bright enough at thinking things out,
but he was hopeless when it came to doing anything.
He was charming as long as you let him talk away on
his own, but if he had to chat with someone else joining in he became so unbearable that it gave one a
headache to listen to him. He was a most loyal friend,
but a most inconsiderate lover. He swore at me and
he also beat me.

TA-SHENG: But you loved him?

PAI-LU (*emphatically*): Yes, I did! When he wanted me
to leave this place and marry him, I did so, and when
he wanted me to go down to the country, I went with
him. He said, "You should have a child," so I had a
child for him. For the first few months after we got
married it was heaven. He loved to see the sunrise, and
every morning he'd get up as soon as it was light and

make me watch the sunrise with him. He was just like a child, so earnest about it all! And so happy! Sometimes he was so pleased about it that he'd turn somersaults in front of me, and he was always saying, "The sun has risen, and the darkness will soon be past." He was the eternal optimist, and he even wrote a novel called *Sunrise*, because he believed that there was hope in everything.

TA-SHENG: But — afterwards?

PAI-LU (*looking in front of her*): Afterwards he began to pursue his hopes alone.

TA-SHENG: How do you mean?

PAI-LU: You wouldn't understand. Afterwards the novelty gradually wore off. The longer we spent together the more dull and dreary it became. I tell you, the most awful thing after marriage is not poverty or jealousy or quarrelling, but dullness, boredom and getting fed up with each other. Both feeling that the other is a burden. We were not interested enough to quarrel any more and we were just wishing the sky would fall one day, waiting to die. At first we just pulled long faces and frowned when we saw each other, and we weren't on speaking terms. In the end he was doing everything he could to make my life a misery, and I was doing the same to him. If he wanted to do anything I tried to stop him, and if I wanted to budge an inch he'd hold me back. It was as if we had been tied together and thrown into the sea, sinking down . . . down . . . down. . . .

TA-SHENG: And yet you both escaped.

PAI-LU: Only because the rope snapped.

TA-SHENG: What do you mean?

PAI-LU: The child died.

TA-SHENG: And so you parted?

PAI-LU: Yes, he went off to pursue his hopes.

TA-SHENG: Where is he now, then?

PAI-LU: No idea.

TA-SHENG: He may always come back to see you one day.

PAI-LU: No, he'll never come back. He's no doubt happy at his work now. (*Her head drooping*) He would think I'd now sunk so low that there was no hope of rescuing me. (*Bitterly*) Hmph! He's forgotten me long ago.

TA-SHENG (*suddenly*): But you don't seem to have forgotten him.

PAI-LU: No, I can't forget him. I won't be able to forget him so long as I live. Here, do you like this? "The sun is risen, and the darkness is left behind; but the sun is not for us, for we shall be asleep." Like it?

TA-SHENG: I'm not quite clear what it means.

PAI-LU: It's said by an old man on his death-bed in his novel.

TA-SHENG: What made you suddenly bring it up?

PAI-LU: Because I . . . I . . . I'm always thinking of people in that situation.

TA-SHENG (*suddenly*): I think you're still in love with him.

PAI-LU (*her head bowed*): Yes, I am.

TA-SHENG: Thank you, Chu-chun, you're a very honest person. (*Getting up*) Well, Chu-chun, I must go and pack now.

PAI-LU: You're not going already? Oh, there's a telegram for you here. (*She takes it out and gives it to him.*)

TA-SHENG (*tearing it open and reading it*): Mm, yes. (*He screws it up into a ball.*)

PAI-LU: Telling you to hurry back home?

TA-SHENG: Yes. (*After a pause*) Well, goodbye, Chu-chun! (*He holds out his hand.*)

PAI-LU: What's all the hurry? You're surely not leaving at the crack of dawn?

TA-SHENG: I intend to leave the hotel at the crack of dawn.

PAI-LU: What train are you getting?

PAI-LU: Who?

HU SZE (*his face as immobile as ever*): The old witch.

PAI-LU: No idea.

HU SZE (*with another yawn*): Tired?

TA-SHENG (*with distaste*): Who do you mean?

HU SZE: Oh, Fang——Mr. Fang. Just got back? Can't get away from each other, can we? Second time we've met tonight.

TA-SHENG (*ignoring him*): Would you like to come and sit in my room, Pai-lu?

PAI-LU: Yes, all right.

(*The two of them go out through the centre door.*)

HU SZE (*watching them out*): Gets on my nerves! A bore and a crank rolled into one.

(*He straightens his clothes, turns towards the mirror again, and pushes the front of his hair into place. He is about to go into the room on the left when — *)

(*The door on the left opens and Pan Yueh-ting and Li Shih-ching appear.*)

LI (*to Pan*): Too crowded in there, we can talk better in here.

PAN: All right, if you like.

HU SZE (*with great familiarity*): You still here, Shih-ching? Not gone home yet?

LI: No. No.

HU SZE: 'Morning, Mr. Pan.

PAN: You'd better hurry, Hu Sze. Mrs. Ku's in there waiting for her opera lesson.

HU SZE: I was just going. Here, Shih-ching, come here a minute. Tell you something.

LI: What is it?

HU SZE (*mischievously*): Saw your wife in the street again yesterday (*in an undertone in Li's ear*), she's not bad!

LI (*having been long accustomed to having Hu Sze speak to him like this, he now finds it difficult to be stiff and*

formal with him.   With embarrassment): What a thing
to say! I'm surprised at you!

HU SZE: Ah, well, must be going.   See you later, Shih-
ching.
*(He goes out in a dandified manner through the door
on the left.)*

PAN: Take a seat.   Something you wanted to see me
about?

LI (*sitting down, very self-satisfied*):   Of course.

PAN: What is it?

LI: Yueh-ting — (*As if finding this name does not come
easily to his tongue*) Do you know what's been happening to the market?

PAN (*pretending*):   Not particularly.   Let's hear it.

LI (*in a low, secretive voice*):   I found all this out from
a very confidential source.   You can set your mind at
rest now: it seems we did the right thing by buying
these bonds. Mr. Chin really is buying this time, and
the rumour that he was trying to start a scare so that
he could unload is quite wrong, pure nervousness.   So
it seems we've done the right thing this time. I've just
worked it out that you're holding four and a half million altogether at the moment, so it looks as if we might
make three hundred thousand on this transaction.

PAN (*pretending to agree with him*):   Yes . . . you're
right . . . yes.
*(But before Li can finish what he is saying he suddenly
interrupts.)*   By the way, I heard Fu-sheng say your
wife —

LI (*who cannot be bothered with such trifles*):   I know,
I know. — As I was saying, it looks as if we might
make three hundred thousand.   That's on the assump-
tion that the prices keep rising at the rate they are
now.   But in a day or two, when people begin to realize
what's happening, the bears will be rushing to cover,
scrambling to pick up what they can, and this will give

a boost to the market. I tell you, within ten days
there'll be a further profit of a hundred or two hundred
thousand for us, just for the picking up, simple as that.

PAN: Yes, yes, but isn't your wife anxious for you to
go home?

LI: Forget her, forget her for the moment. What I suggest, Yueh-ting, is that we shouldn't on any account
sell our holdings now. I tell you, this time the prices
are going to go up and up and up, not just rise so far
and then stop. In fact (*very excited*), if you'll take
my advice, Yueh-ting, the best thing we can do is to
buy more as we see fit tomorrow. There'll still be time
to buy some more tomorrow without losing on them.

PAN: Shih-ching, do you realize that your son's ill?

LI: That's all right, don't worry about that — (*More
excited than ever*) I think we should go on buying. Yes!
That's settled, then. This is the chance of a lifetime,
Yueh-ting. When we've pulled this off successfully I
don't think the bank should take any more risks of
this kind. Whatever happens we should never act in
such an unethical manner again: in future we must
keep faith with our investors. But this time, now that
we've burnt our boats, we should have a look at the
market first thing in the morning and buy up some
more.

PAN: But —

LI: We should take a further half a million to make it
up to a round figure. Can't go wrong, I should say.
The way I've been working it out, the first thing that
we should do is to put the bank's credit on a firm footing, which means: first, the deposits should be —

PAN: Shih-ching! I do think you'd best go home and
see how things are. Don't you realize your son's seriously ill?

LI: Why must you keep on bringing that up?

PAN: I think you're being too cheerful.

LI: Yes, I am. I think I've helped you handle this bit of business in a way that does us credit. Naturally I'm cheerful!

PAN (*with a sardonic smile*): I'm sorry, I was forgetting that you've been my assistant for the last two days.

LI: What do you mean, sir?

PAN (*ignoring his question*): Mr. Li, these bonds I'm holding are now money?

LI: Of course.

PAN: And this little bit of profit will be enough to repay Mr. Chin's loan in full?

LI: According to my reckoning there'll be some over.

PAN: Excellent. Now, think: with this surplus, plus such influence and ability as I possess, is it likely that I'm going to stand for any nonsense from anybody?

LI: I'm afraid I don't quite see what you're driving at, sir.

PAN: It's possible that someone might start putting it around that my bank has insufficient reserves —

LI: Eh?

PAN: Or go round saying I've mortgaged all the bank's property.

LI (*with an ingratiating smile*): What's the point of going into all this, sir? It's not —

PAN: I've no wish to bring the subject up, but there's always a chance that someone else will insist on bringing it up.

LI: That's rather far-fetched, sir.

PAN (*looking at him coldly*): Only six or seven days ago you yourself were saying it to my face, Mr. Li.

LI: Now, don't vex yourself over it, sir. To quote the Classics: "If one is not patient in small things one will never be able to control great ventures." It would always seem better for a man in charge of great affairs to be patient, rather than impatient.

PAN *(with a glare at him):* I think I've been patient enough these last few days. Let me tell you quite plainly, though, I dislike intensely having a self-opinionated person keep blowing his own trumpet to me; and I don't very much like having people think I'm easy meat, and imagining that I'm going to submit willingly to blackmail. What is most detestable is when my colleagues in the bank call me a blind old fool behind my back because I get an uneducated third-rater as my assistant.

LI *(controlling himself with a great effort):* It wouldn't hurt you to be a little more polite, sir. You might weigh your words a shade more carefully before coming out with them.

PAN: I've weighed my words with the greatest care.

LI *(with a mirthless smile):* All right, then; the actual words you've been using are not so very important. After all, first-raters and third-raters are much the same, very little difference really. The point is, sir, we're both men with a good proportion of public responsibilities, and I think the least one can do, whether on large issues or small ones, is to keep one's word.

PAN: Keep one's word? *(Laughing aloud)* Is that what you're worried about, keeping one's word? It's not that I never keep my word, but it depends who to. And after being around all these years I ought to know who to keep my word to and who not.

LI: Then it appears, sir, that you're not prepared to keep your word to me.

PAN *(acidly):* That's not the sort of remark one would have expected from a clever man like you.

LI: Well, of course, you're much cleverer than the rest of us, sir.

PAN: Not necessarily. But it may be that I do have one small streak of common-sense on one important point: I may sometimes utterly refuse to keep my word to

self-opinionated scoundrels. (*Suddenly*) Do you realize
that your wife has been phoning you?

LI (*confused*): I know, I know.

PAN: Your son's seriously ill, dying. Mrs. Li wants you
home urgently.

LI (*glaring angrily at Pan*): I'm going right away.

PAN: I'm glad to hear it. Your car's waiting for you
outside. (*Harshly*) It won't take you long to get home
by car. When you get home you might get in a bit of
practice with your cleverness. I can't see a shrewd,
go-ahead man like you being without a job. When you
do get a job, I suppose you can always open people's
drawers, in order to see, for example, whether their
property has been mortgaged or not, or to check up on
the actual amount of their deposits. — Oh, I might as
well tell you, while we're on the subject, that in order
to spare you any further anxiety on my account I've
now taken the documents out of the drawer and put
them in the safe.

LI (*staring and gaping*): Oh!

PAN (*taking an envelope out of his pocket*): This, Mr.
Li, is the outstanding part of your salary. Let's just
work it out. The salary of a director's assistant is two
hundred and seventy-five dollars a month. You were on
this job for three days, and the accountant tells me
you've already drawn an advance of two hundred and
fifty dollars on it, but I think we ought to treat you
decently, so I'm paying you a full month's salary. So
please accept the remaining twenty-five dollars.
Though the bank won't be able to pay the bill for the
car you've been using today.

LI: But Mr. Pan— (*He suddenly breaks off and holds
out his hand, glaring at Pan with hatred.*) All right,
give it here, then.

(*He takes the money.*)

PAN (*lighting a cigar*): Well, I'll be off now. Drop in
for a chat any time you're free. And you can call me

what you please, Yueh-ting if you like; you can drop
the sirs and call me "old chap" if you like, now that
we're on an equal footing! Goodbye.   (*He goes out
left.*)

LI (*numb with rage*):   All right, then! (*Clutching the
notes tightly, his voice low with indignation*) Twenty-
five dollars! (*His voice sinking even lower*) Twenty-
five dollars.   (*Grinding his teeth*) I could smash you
for this! (*The telephone rings but he ignores it.*) For
the sake of these few bonds of yours I even put my
family out of my mind, I even ignore my child's illness,
I spend my salary on bribes to get information for
you.   But now that you've succeeded and made your
money, you're suddenly finished with me. (*With
a mirthless smile*) Finished with me. You treat me like
a thief, you call me names to my face, insult me, look
down on me! (*Struck where it hurts most, raising his
voice*) Yes, you look down on me! (*Pounding his chest*)
You look down on Li Shih-ching. Yes, you had me on
a piece of string this time, all right. (*The telephone
rings again. He laughs shrilly, mocking himself*) So
I'm a "self-opinionated person!" I'm "uneducated!"
I'm a "scoundrel," a "third-rater!" (*An unnatural laugh,
then the telephone rings again.*) And you think I'm
going to let you get away with it just like that? Think
I'm afraid of you? — Huh! (*His eyes flashing with indignation*) Today I'm going to finish you off, the whole
gang of you. I won't leave one of you standing, not a
single one of you.

(*Suddenly there is an urgent knocking on the centre
door.*)

LI: Who is it?

(*Mrs. Li comes in in great agitation. She looks more
haggard than ever. Her clothing is rumpled and her
eyes are filled with tears.*)

MRS. LI: Shih-ching! What's got into you? You've
been out all day and still you're not home!

LI (*looking fixedly at her*): I'm not going home!

MRS. LI (*breaking down*): It'll soon be all over with little Wu, his tongue's gone cold already, Shih-ching. I got a car and Mother and I have been to three hospitals with him, but none of them will take him.

LI: Won't take him? Is he past treating, then?

MRS. LI: They want money. They all want cash down, no credit. Even the cheapest one wants fifty dollars deposit. And all we've got in the house is fifteen, so if I spend our last penny it still won't be enough. (*Sobbing*) Shih-ching, you must find a way of saving him.

LI (*feeling in his pockets and producing a few small notes*): Here, take the lot.

MRS. LI (*hurriedly counting them*): There's — there's only seventeen dollars and a bit here.

LI: Then — in that case there's nothing we can do.

MRS. LI (*wiping her eyes*): Shih-ching (*looking at him*), our little Wu —

LI (*indignantly*): Why did we have to go and have all these children? (*Nevertheless he finds himself picking up the notes he has just been given, clutching them tightly in his hand. Then, swallowing his resentment, he hands them to his wife, his voice full of bitterness.*) Take it, take it! Twenty-five dollars, the price of my self-respect.

MRS. LI (*quickly taking the money, urgently*): Aren't you coming with me?

LI: You go on ahead. I'll be along later.

MRS. LI: You can't do that! You must come with me!

LI (*bellowing*): When I tell you to go on ahead, you go on ahead. Don't stand there arguing! Go on, get a move on! Don't get me riled!

(*A knock on the door.*)

MRS. LI (*imploring him*): Shih-ching — (*Another knock on the door.*)

LI: Who is it?

(No reply. Another knock.)

LI: Come in! Who is it?

(No reply. Another knock.)

LI *(explosively)*: Who is it? Come in! *(He goes across to the centre door and pulls it violently open.)*

(Huang Hsing-san stands like a skeleton in the doorway, looking at him with glittering eyes.)

LI *(surprised, in a low voice)*: So it's you!

(He brings his dismal presence into the room, like the chill breath of a sad wind. His present appearance makes one think of a ghost, of one of the cold dead creeping from the tomb at midnight. His gown has disappeared. Above the waist he wears only a tattered wadded jacket of a blue that is almost black, with the collar unbuttoned to reveal the jutting bones of his neck. Below this jacket there is only an unlined pair of trousers. His hair is thoroughly dishevelled and his body is more hunched than ever, though he does not seem so timid as last time. His face is dispirited and expressionless. He gazes dully at Li Shih-ching as if possessed by an evil spirit.)

LI *(to his wife)*: You'd better go. Somebody here.

MRS. LI: Shih-ching — you. . . . *(Throwing him a complaining look, she goes out whimpering through the centre door.)*

LI *(watching her out, angrily)*: Hmph, I'm not going. I'm not going. I'll die before I leave here without finding a way to get even with him. *(He paces to and fro, forgetting that Huang Hsing-san is with him.)*

HUANG: Mr. Pan, sir!

LI *(stopping in his tracks)*: You — you tramp.

HUANG: Mr. Pan!

LI *(suspicious)*: What do you mean, "Mr. Pan"? What's the idea of calling me Mr. Pan?

HUANG *(still woodenly as if reciting a text from memory)*: Mr. Pan, I'm a petty clerk at the bank. My

name's Huang, Huang Hsing-san, and I earn ten dollars
twenty-five cents a month. I've three children, sir. . .
and I earn ten dollars twenty-five a month!

LI (*looking at him and suddenly understanding*): You!
You're — (*With distaste*) What are you coming round
after me again for?

HUANG: Mr. Pan! I beg you, I beg you!

LI (*irascibly*): Mr. Pan be damned! My name's not Pan,
it's Li! (*Pointing to himself*) Surely you know me?
Don't you?

HUANG (*nodding*): Yes, I know you. I know you, Mr.
Pan.

LI: Bah! What's the matter with you? Why do you have
to choose this of all times to come to make fun of me?

HUANG (*still in the same dull voice*): They won't let
me die! They won't agree to let me die.

LI: You can die if you like.

HUANG: But the officials and the other gentlemen,
they insisted on letting me go. They insisted that my
mind was deranged at the time. They insisted that I
was innocent. (*Earnestly*) I beg of you, please, do me
one favour; punch me again hard (*indicating the re-
gion of his lungs*), here; just one punch, please, Mr.
Pan, please.

LI (*raising his voice*): Didn't you hear me? My name
isn't Pan. Now have a good look at me. My name's
not Pan, it's Li, Li Shih-ching.
(*A pause.*)

HUANG (*suddenly beginning to whimper like a woman*):
My children, my poor children, I killed you, your
daddy made you die.

LI: You mean your children are all —

HUANG: All gone to heaven. (*Suddenly*) Why won't
you let me die? (*His mind is wandering and he thinks
he is still in the courtroom.*) I'm not insane! I tell you,
Your Honour, I'm really not insane. My mind was

quite clear, I bought the opium myself out of the three
dollars that Mr. Pan gave me: two dollars went on
the rent and the other one on the opium. Your Honour,
I bought the brown sugar myself to mix with
it. I made the children take it, I poisoned them with
my own hands. Why couldn't you let me jump in the
river? I'd no money to buy any more opium. Why
won't you let me die? My mind's quite clear, I'm not
in the least bit insane. The law's the law, you can't
just let me go. *(Grasping Li by the hand)* Your Honour,
I've committed murder with my own hands, I've
poisoned my children, my Wang, my little Yun, my.
. . . *(Throwing his arms round Li)* Put me to death,
Your Honour!

LI *(struggling free with a violent effort):* Get away,
take your hands off me, you stupid idiot! Look where
you are. *(Shaking him violently)* Look at me, who am
I?

HUANG *(looking first at Li, then all round the room,
he pauses for a moment. Suddenly)*: Mr. — Mr. Pan,
what is this place I've come to?

LI: Bah! What do you keep pestering me for, you bag
of bones! Go on, out, clear out, or else I'll send for the
police to take you away.
(He goes to press a bell.)

HUANG: No, don't, don't send for the police. *(In an
anguished voice)* Mr. Pan, human beings can't treat
each other like this, they just can't! A few days ago my
children were alive and I wanted to keep alive; I
begged you to let me stay alive, but you wouldn't. Now
(weeping) they're dead, now I want to die. I'm begging
you to let me die and you won't let me. We're all
human beings, Mr. Pan. Human beings can't treat
each other like this! *(Hopelessly)* They can't treat each
other like this!

LI: Bah! . . . You stupid idiot! You give me the jitters. Get out, get out (*stamping his foot repeatedly*), before you drive me mad as well. Out, you tramp, right out.

HUANG: No, please, Mr. Pan, have a heart. I can't go on living any longer. (*He sinks to his knees, buries his face in his hands and sobs bitterly.*)

LI (*pulling him up*): All right, I will, I'll let you die. But first get up. First of all you must realize who I am. My name's Li. Now listen carefully once more: my name's Li. Li, Li, Li.

HUANG (*unable to recall the name*): Li?

LI: Don't you remember coming here to see me the other day? . . . When I . . . I advised you to go rickshaw-pulling?

HUANG: Yes?

LI: And I also advised you to beg?

HUANG: Yes?

LI: And I also advised you to steal?

HUANG: That's it, you also advised me to throw myself off the top of a building! (*With a sudden frenzied delight he looks all round and as his eye falls on the window he runs straight over to it.*)

LI (*running after him and holding him with one hand while shouting towards the door*): Fu-sheng! Fu-sheng!

(*Fu-sheng comes in through the centre door.*)

LI: Bundle him outside. He's mad.

FU-SHENG (*putting his arms round Huang's waist*): You back again!

(*He begins dragging Huang outside by main force. Huang struggles ineffectually.*)

HUANG: Mr. Li, I'm not mad! I'm not mad!

(*He is dragged outside by Fu-sheng.*)

LI: My God! (*Indignantly*) You stupid bastard, why go mad? Why let yourself be driven mad? You let him off too easily! (*The telephone rings urgently again.*)

LI (*picking up the receiver*): Hullo? Who? Mr. Chang at
the newspaper offices? Oh, this is Shih-ching. What?
You rang a short while ago? What about? Oh . . . I
see . . . you've already sent a note round by hand.
I see. . . . What? Bad news? Who says so? . . . You
mean it was also leaked out by Chin's people? Impossible! But these past few days we've been hearing
that Chin's been buying himself! . . . Eh? He hasn't
bought a thing? . . . Ah, so the rise we've been expecting this week is nothing more than one of his
rumours. . . . Eh? He started getting rid of his holdings
yesterday?. . . Is that really true? (*Beaming with
delight*) What? So the news is already going round, is
it? . . . Yes, yes, that means the market will start
dropping fast tomorrow as soon as the session opens.
By the way, how much do you think it'll drop by?. . .
(*Slapping the table*) What? They'll close in the second
session? (*Sitting down on the table*) Ah . . . I see . . .
(*slapping his buttocks*). You say that. . . . The Ta
Feng Bank's been taken in nicely by Chin over these
bonds, you say. . . . Yes . . . yes, that's what I think.
Chances are Chin'll be demanding his deposit back.
. . . Jolly good — I mean it's a great blow. Right you
are . . . yes, I see, the note's already been sent round
here by hand. Right, see you later. Yes, I'll let Mr.
Pan have it. (*He replaces the receiver and goes hurriedly to the door.*)

LI: Fu-sheng, Fu-sheng!
(*Fu-sheng comes in.*)

LI: Mr. Chang at the newspaper offices sent a messenger
round with a note for Mr. Pan a short while ago. Have
you seen it?

FU-SHENG: Yes, it came some time ago.

LI: Where is it?

FU-SHENG: Here it is. (*He produces it from a pocket.*)

LI: Give it here, man! Why didn't you say anything about it before? *(He snatches it from Fu-sheng's hand and hurriedly reads it.)*

FU-SHENG *(giving his explanation while Li is reading)*: I was going to give it to Mr. Pan a moment ago, but I found him busy playing mahjong. He was doing very well and he had a winning hand, so I didn't disturb him.

LI: Oh, go away! Get out! Don't stand there drivelling.

FU-SHENG: Very good, sir. *(He goes out.)*

LI *(beside himself with excitement)*: You've come just right! Just right! You couldn't have come at a better moment.

(Pai-lu comes in through the centre door.)

LI *(his face wreathed in smiles)*: Ah, Miss Chen.

PAI-LU: Mr. Li. Won't you sit down?

LI: Have your visitors gone yet?

PAI-LU: They'll be going any minute now.

LI: If you're just going in there, Miss, I wonder if I could trouble you to ask Mr. Pan to come out here for a moment as soon as he can. There's a note here for him that's just been brought round, something extremely important has happened. So could you ask him to come out at once and give instructions on what should be done about it?

PAI-LU: But of course, Mr. Li. Though won't you sit down till he comes?

LI: Thank you, yes. *(He bows.)*

(Pai-lu goes out left.)

LI *(trembling with excitement)*: Ah . . . oh . . . I must get a firm hold on myself. *(He paces up and down.)*

(Pan Yueh-ting comes in from the left.)

PAN: Oh, haven't you gone home yet?

LI: No, sir, I can't tear myself away all the time I'm worrying about your bank's affairs.

PAN: What did you want me for?

LI *(in a low, self-effacing voice):* How's your game
  going?

PAN *(looking at him):* Not too badly at all!

LI: I hear you're in good form tonight.

PAN: Not bad, I must admit. Where's the note?

LI: Note?

PAN *(annoyed):* Yes, where's this note?

LI: Which note?

PAN: Pai-lu said you had a note in your hand addressed
  to me.

LI: Oh, yes, of course. From Mr. Chang at the newspaper offices. He sent it round by hand.

PAN: Give it to me, then. *(To himself)* Surely the
  bonds can't be — *(To Li)* Let's have it, then.

LI: It's about the bonds, of course. It came as a very
  great surprise to me when I saw what was in it.

PAN: How do you know what it's about?

LI: The same way as before, sir. I opened it and read
  it without waiting for you.

PAN *(suppressing his indignation with an effort):* I'm
  surprised that you should open a letter addressed to
  me. Give it to me.

LI *(with an ingratiating smile):* If I didn't open it, how
  would I know whether it was good news or not, and
  how I should break it to you? *(Drawing it slowly from
  his pocket)* You won't be angry with me? You won't
  say I'm self-opinionated or over-inquisitive? *(He takes
  the note out of the envelope with deliberate slowness
  and spreads it out on the table.)* Read it carefully,
  sir.
  *(Pan seems to sense that there is something unusual
  behind all this. He looks distrustfully at Li, then hastily picks up the note.)*

LI *(hesitantly):* It's a thing I'd never expected; things
  just don't work out as neatly as this; it's too easy to be
  true. I'm certain it's all a rumour.

PAN *(a great change coming over his face as he finishes reading the letter):* I — I don't believe it. It's not true. *(Reading the letter again)* This information can't be reliable. *(Hurriedly going to the telephone and dialling a number)* Hullo, is that Hsin Pao News? My name's Pan, Pan Yueh-ting. . . . I want to speak to the editor, Mr. Chang. And hurry, it's urgent! . . . What? He's gone out? But a moment ago he. . . . Oh, I see, he went out just this minute. Do you know where he's gone? . . . You don't know? . . . Why didn't you ask him, you idiot? . . . *(He replaces the receiver and pauses a moment before dialling another number.)* Hullo, Hui Hsien Club? I want to speak to Mr. Ting. . . . Mr. Chin's private secretary, Mr. Ting Mu-chih. . . . What? Gone home? How could he have gone already? It's now only *(looking at his wristwatch)* only —

LI: It's now only just after five. It'll soon be light.

PAN *(glancing at Li):* What's his home number, then? . . . 43543, yes . . . all right. . . . *(Replacing the receiver)* Awkward lot, you can never find them when you want them in a hurry. *(Dialling another number)* Hullo . . . hullo . . . hullo, is that Mr. Ting's residence? Hullo . . . hullo . . . hullo. *(To himself)* How can there be no reply?

LI: The servants are probably all asleep by now.

PAN *(slamming the receiver down):* They must sleep like the dead! *(Sitting down weakly)* It's nonsense! Nonsense! His information can't be reliable. It's impossible. Impossible.

(Li Shih-ching fixes his gloating eyes unwaveringly upon him.)

(Pai-lu comes in left and glances at the pair of them.)

PAN: Could I bother you to get me a glass of water?

PAI-LU: What's the matter?

PAN: I've got a bit of a headache.

(Pai-lu goes across to get the water.)

LI: I agree his information must be unreliable. (*With an assumed earnestness*) You hadn't heard anything of the kind up to this morning, had you!

PAN (*to himself*): He's pulling my leg.   He must be pulling my leg.

PAI-LU (*handing him a glass of water*): What's the matter, Yueh-ting?

PAN: This note, look at it! (*He sits there bemused.*)

LI (*going over to Pan and lowering his voice*): In actual fact, sir, it wouldn't be such a terrible blow. You wouldn't lose all that amount even if prices did drop a couple of cents. Did you read the letter carefully, sir, to see whether it actually said how big the drop would be?

PAN (*suddenly rising*): Ah, yes. Lulu, give me the note. (*He snatches it from her and hurriedly reads it.*)

LI (*standing behind him and pointing*): No, not there, it's on this page, here.

LI & PAN (*reading the note in low voices*): ". . . This information has already got round, and prices are bound to make a sudden steep plunge tomorrow. No doubt about it. . . ."

PAI-LU: He says quite plainly that there's bound to be a complete slump.

PAN (*staring dazedly at the note*): Yes. His idea is that they'll close trading as soon as the session opens tomorrow.

LI: After Mr. Chang had sent the note, he also phoned.

PAN (*seeing a gleam of hope*): He phoned? Well, what did he say?

LI: He said there was nothing we could do about it. Mr. Chin's behind the scenes pulling the strings, so there's not the slightest thing we can do.

PAN (*brokenly*): The swine!

(*Fu-sheng pushes open the centre door and comes in.*)

PAI-LU: What is it?

FU-SHENG: Mr. Chang from the newspaper's here.

PAI-LU: Ask him in.

FU-SHENG: He says there are too many people over here, so he's waiting in number ten.

(*Pan Yueh-ting at once makes for the door.*)

(*Almost at the same moment as Fu-sheng comes in the telephone rings.*)

LI (*answering the telephone*): Hullo, who is it? . . . This is number fifty-two. Oh . . . this is Shih-ching. . . . Oh, you want Mr. Pan? He's here now. (*Stopping Pan*) Mr. Chin's secretary, Mr. Ting wants to speak to you.

PAN (*hurriedly taking the receiver from him*): Mr. Ting? Yueh-ting here. I've been hunting high and low for you . . . yes . . . yes . . . yes . . . not at all. . . . What! He wants to withdraw it. . . . What! The whole lot, tomorrow morning? Yes, but listen, it was clearly agreed between Mr. Chin and me that it would be extended a further week. . . . Then he's . . . why, he must be pulling my leg, that's all I can say! . . . (*Exasperatedly*) Now listen, Mr. Ting. He can't go back on his word like this. . . . He gave me his word, tell him. He agreed to give me another week, and now he suddenly turns round and. . . . Now listen . . . listen . . . I'd be obliged if he'd have a word with me. What? He's not seeing anyone just now? . . . Listen, tell me this, Mu-chih: has Mr. Chin bought any government bonds the last few days? . . . What? . . . He can't get rid of them fast enough? . . . I see. . . . Hullo! Hullo! . . . (*He rattles the receiver-rest up and down but can get no reply. He replaces the receiver.*) Bastard, leaves it till this time of morning before he tells me. (*He collapses exhaustedly into a chair.*)

FU-SHENG: Sir, Mr. Chang's. . . .

PAN: Oh, get out! And don't come bothering me again, any of you.

(*Fu-sheng goes out.*)

LI: But, sir —

PAN (*bellowing*): Go on, get away! (*To Li Shih-ching*) Go away, I say!

(*Li goes out through the centre door.*)

PAN (*to Pai-lu*): If you'll just leave me alone here to have a rest. . . .

PAI-LU: Yueh-ting, you —

PAN (*with a wave of his hand*): You'd better go and see your guests. They're probably ready to go.

(*Pai-lu goes out left.*)

PAN (*pacing to and fro, too restless to sit or stand still*): The laugh's on me this time. I can see Chin's determined to settle my hash once and for all.

(*The centre door opens slightly.*)

PAN (*startled*): Who is it?

LI: Me, sir. The self-opinionated scoundrel back again.

PAN: What — what do you want?

LI: I thought it would be more satisfactory for the two of us to talk alone.

PAN: What more is there to talk about?

LI: Nothing. Just a third-rater coming to see how the first-rater's getting along now.

PAN (*springing to his feet*): You scoundrel!

LI (*his eyebrows shooting up*): Scoundrel yourself!

PAN: Clear out!

LI (*in equally violent tones*): You clear out yourself! (*A pause; then, with a mocking smile*) You're forgetting that we're on an equal footing now.

PAN (*calming himself with an effort and sitting down*): You'd better watch your step, speaking like this.

LI: I've no need to watch my step. I haven't a penny to my name and my pockets are full of pawn tickets. No need for me to watch my step!

PAN: You'd better watch out somebody doesn't invite you to answer a lawsuit, you pauper.

LI: As you say, a pauper. But before you say that you'd better have a look at yourself, my dear Mr. Pan. I'm not in debt, I'm not tens of thousands of dollars

in debt. I haven't got people pressing me for money.
I haven't had money snatched from under my very
nose just as I was thinking it was mine. You'd better
start feeling sorry for yourself, Mr. Pan. You don't
even qualify as a pauper. I was made a fool of by a
scoundrel, and I'm just poor, but you've been made a
fool of by an even greater scoundrel, and he's after
your blood! (*Bitingly*) Yes, you wouldn't keep your
word to a self-opinionated scoundrel, and now you've
been paid in your own coin! You may go back on
your word, but other people can beat you at it. You
thought you were clever, but somebody was cleverer
than you were! You called me names, you made fun
of me. You insulted me, yes, and despised me, too.
(*Raising his voice*) But now I'm very happy, very
glad! Tomorrow morning I'll be able to watch the
rush on your bank with my own eyes, I'll see you
unable to pay up, I'll see the small savers who've nine
or ten dollars apiece in your bank, calling you names,
cursing you — yes, they'll lynch you, they'll eat you
alive! You've ruined them! You've ruined them, and
they'll flay the skin off your back, they'll gouge out
your heart! The only thing that can satisfy them now
is your death! Death is your only escape!

PAN (*banging the table with exasperation*): Stop it!
Stop it!

LI: No, I'll have my say out — you doddering old fool,
you born mug, blind and muddle-headed —

PAN (*springing up*): I'll — I'll kill you! Here and now!
(*He grapples with Li, seizes him by the throat, and is
about to —*)
(*Pai-lu bursts in.*)

PAI-LU: Yueh-ting! Yueh-ting! Let go of him!

LI (*struggling, with Pan still clutching his throat*): Kill
me, then! Kill me! But Chin won't let you get away:
outside . . . outside. . . .

PAI-LU: Let him go, Yueh-ting.

PAN (*thrusting him away, raising his voice*): What about outside?

LI: What about it? Outside Black San's waiting for you.

PAN: Why — what for?

LI: Mr. Chin's sent him to keep an eye on you. He's afraid you might try to escape.

(*There is a pause while Pan bows his head.*)

PAI-LU (*in an undertone*): You'd better go now, Mr. Li.

PAN (*suddenly to Li with a dismal grin*): I suppose you're satisfied now!

(*Li looks at him but does not speak.*)

(*The telephone rings urgently.*)

PAN: Take it for me, Pai-lu.

LI: Let me take it.

PAI-LU: No, no, I'll get it. (*She has already picked up the receiver, and Li and Pan stand either side of her, looking tensely at her.*) Hullo, who is it? This is suite fifty-two, Chen Pai-lu. Ah, Mrs. Li. I see . . . you want Mr. Li? He's here now. (*Turning to Li*) It's Mrs. Li, phoning from the hospital.

LI (*taking the receiver*): Shih-ching here. You got to the hospital, then? Oh, I see . . . little Wu's what? (*Agitatedly, in complete contrast to his unconcern of a moment ago*) What? Say it again . . . I can't hear very well. . . . What! Little Wu's passed . . . passed out? Then — then get a doctor! (*Slapping the table in his anguish*) Get a doctor! You've got the money with you, haven't you? Pay them! Give them the money! . . . What? He . . . he died on the . . . on the way? . . . (*The tears running down his cheeks*) Calling "Daddy" . . . and then . . . (*He lets the receiver fall and begins to sob.*) Oh, my boy! My little Wu. (*Suddenly picking up the receiver again*) I'm coming over! Straight over!

(*As Li Shih-ching snatches up his hat he looks at Pan while wiping his eyes. Pan returns him a dazed glance, then Li goes out through the centre door.*)

PAI-LU (*watching Li out, then turning to Pan*): What
    was all that about, Yueh-ting?
    (*A cock crows in the distance.*)
PAN: Your visitors gone, Pai-lu?
PAI-LU: Yes, some time ago. There's only Hu Sze and
    Mrs. Ku still here.
PAN: To think that I should ever live through such a
    day! If you'll wait a moment, Pai-lu, I think I'll go
    and talk things over with Mr. Chang from the news-
    paper.
PAI-LU: Feel better now, Yueh-ting?
PAN: Well enough. I'll be off now. I'll be back later
    on.
PAI-LU: Are you leaving me now?
PAN: No, I'll be back later.
PAI-LU: All right, off you go, then.
    (*Pan goes out through the centre door.*)
    (*Again a cock crows in the distance.*)
PAI-LU (*in a low, sad voice*): It'll soon be morning again.
    (*Hu Sze and Mrs. Ku come in through the door on the
    left. Hu Sze's face is glowing with the exhilaration
    of an opium smoker. He continues with what he is
    saying while wiping his face with his hand. Mrs. Ku
    follows him in, worshipping her hero.*)
HU SZE (*sighing contentedly*): Not a bad drop of opium,
    that. It's really pepped me up! (*Continuing what he
    was saying before*) Then straight after that comes the
    introduction on the drum. And the large gong and the
    small one both join in: *ba-la-da-chang, ba-la-da-chang,
    ba-la-da-chang, chang-chang-ling-chang, ba-la-da, da,
    da* . . . (*He coughs and spits on the floor.*)
MRS. KU: Spitting again! Come on, teach me it prop-
    erly. (*Quite unconscious of Pai-lu's state of mind
    at the moment, proudly*) Listen, Lulu. Listen to Hu
    Sze teaching me *Staying the Night and Killing Hsichiao*.
    (*Showing off*) That introduction was called "the rush-
    ing wind."

HU SZE (*his voice thick and hoarse from too much opium, yet very vivaciously, rolling his eyes in despair*): "Rushing wind," she says! You'll never learn opera if your memory's as bad as that.

MRS. KU (*trying to cover up*): No, I mean it's the "long slow stabs."

HU SZE: Oh, go on, forget it! It's not called the "long slow stabs." Now let's get on with it. It'll be enough if you just pay attention to the rhythm of it: (*repeating it*) *ba-la-da-chang, ba-la-da-chang, ba-la-da-chang, chang-chang-ling-chang. Ba-la-da!* (*He suddenly stops, then, with great panache, he strikes downwards three times with his right hand to represent the drum.*) *Da! Da! Da!* (*Then a downward blow for the gong*) *Chang!* (*His whole body alive, his face reflecting the enthusiasm with which he is throwing himself into the part, his words tumbling out with great rapidity*) Now, watch: after the introduction the old man swings his beard, knits his brows, glares, quivering all over. Then the drum gives him his accompaniment and the old man grinds his teeth, points, and shouts (*his pointing finger almost touching the tip of Mrs. Ku's nose*): "You cheap jade! . . ."

MRS. KU: Can't we have something else beside "cheap jades" all the time? I don't want to hear the "old man" parts: it's the soubrette parts that I'm studying.

HU SZE (*contemptuously*): Soubrette? You? (*A pause*) All right, then, but you'll have to tell me which passage you want to do.

MRS. KU (*appearing to rack her brains*): That bit that goes "Suddenly I hear . . ." or whatever it is, after the part where somebody sings "I'll ask her to open the door."

HU SZE: Oh, that's simple, that's an easy bit!

MRS. KU: Let's see you sing it with all the actions, then.

HU SZE: Easy. Nothing to it. Fiddle playing the *Szeping* melody: *yi-ge-lung-ge-li-ge-lung-ge-lung-ge-*

lung. Sing: *(with liberal bodily movement)* "I will ask
her to open the door!" Back to speak voice: "My dear
young lady, come and let me in!"

MRS. KU: I want the soubrette part.

HU SZE: Don't get impatient! Immediately afterwards,
the curtain is lifted aside, and the soubrette comes on.
(Mincing and posturing with a handkerchief in his hand)
Your steps must be light and graceful, your eyes lively,
and when you come out on to the stage you strike a
pose — the audience likes a bit of swank! Like this!
(Looking coy and inviting) Yi-ge-lung-ge-li-ge-lung-ge-
lung-ge-lung. (In a falsetto) "Suddenly I hear" — *(going*
back to his normal voice) lung-ge-li-ge-lung-ge-lung-
ge-lung-ge-lung — *(throwing himself into it whole-*
heartedly) "someone calling me outside the door." *Lung-*
ge-lung-li-ge-lung-ge-go-lung-ge. . . .
(A cock crows in the distance.)

PAI-LU *(lost in reverie)*: Listen, listen to that.

HU SZE *(still keeping his pose)*: What?

PAI-LU: A cock crowing.
(The cock crows again in the distance.)

MRS. KU: Why, so it is! *(Suddenly looking out of the*
window) Why, it'll soon be light. *(To Hu Sze)* Come
on, we must be going! Time for bed. We've been
here longer than usual tonight.

HU SZE *(with an air of complete unconcern)*: By the
way, what about that bill of mine for five hundred
dollars?

MRS. KU: I'll make out a cheque on the Ta Feng Bank
as soon as I get home. Though you —

HU SZE *(acquiescently)*: I'll be good. No more going
to see that bad woman.

MRS. KU: Now then, don't start making a fool of yourself in front of Lulu. Hurry up and get your things
on and we'll be going. Now tomorrow — or rather
today, you've got to go to the studios to shoot a film,
haven't you?

HU SZE (*the perfect yes-man, lying easily*): Yes, I have. The director said if I didn't turn up today they couldn't shoot it.

MRS. KU: Then hurry up and get your things on and get home to bed. I'm going with you to the studios myself today to have a look round.

HU SZE (*taken aback*): Oh, are you? I — er. . . . (*But he prefers to pass the subject over for the moment: slowly and with infinite care he puts his coat on.*)

MRS. KU (*turning to Pai-lu, very well pleased with herself*): You know, Lulu, Hu Sze's going to be a great film-star. In no time at all he'll be a great success. The Company says he's a unique, unprecedented *chef d'oeuvre*, and they want him to do three films in a row. In a few days' time the film magazines will be printing his picture. And they may be printing mine, too.

PAI-LU: Yours?

MRS. KU: Yes, mine, one of me and Hu Sze. One of Mrs. Ku with Hu Sze, that great star of the screen, the greatest in China. You see (*lowering her voice and speaking with shyness and embarrassment, like a little girl*) I'm going to . . . I'm now going to accept him after all. I'm hoping . . . I'm hoping that the day after tomorrow we'll . . . we'll be getting married. There, Lulu, don't you think that will be nice?

PAI-LU: Yes, very nice. But —

MRS. KU: Lulu, you'll be one of the bridesmaids, now don't say you won't.

PAI-LU (*her voice becoming lower*): All right, then, but —

MRS. KU (*giving Pai-lu a playful smack*): Go on with you, you and your 'buts'!

PAI-LU: I was going to ask whether your money is in the Ta Feng Bank at the moment.

MRS. KU: Of course it is. Why do you ask?

PAI-LU: Oh, nothing. Just thought I'd ask.

MRS. KU (*gazing at Hu Sze in admiration*): Ah! (*She opens her bag and takes out a powder-compact. She is just going to begin making up her face when she catches sight of the bottle of sleeping-tablets.*) Look at that, Lulu! I don't know what I'm keeping these for! (*Taking the bottle out of the bag*) I'd better give them back to you. I shan't need them now, thanks all the same.

PAI-LU: Thank you. (*Taking them*) I was just going to ask you for them back.

MRS. KU: Good, I'd rather you kept them.

HU SZE (*now dressed up and ready to go*): Come on, then, let's go.

MRS. KU: Don't rush me. I've still got to do my face yet.

HU SZE (*grasping her by the arm*): Oh, skip it. Who's going to see you at this time of morning? Come on, let's go! (*He steers her towards the centre door.*)

MRS. KU (*to Pai-lu, proudly*): See the way he bosses me around? (*As Hu Sze drags her another step or two*) Goodbye, then!

HU SZE: Cheerio, Pai-lu.

(*Hu Sze puts on his hat and tugs the brim down, then departs with Mrs. Ku through the centre door.*)

(*Left alone, Pai-lu goes to the window and opens it. In the stillness the outlines of the buildings opposite can be seen emerging slowly from the darkness. Everything is the same as in Act One: outside is a world of stillness and solitude, and faintly from a great distance comes the sound of a factory hooter, mingling with the crowing of cocks that is heard now and then from the market. It is the hour when darkness gives way to the glow of morning, before the sun has appeared.*)

(*There is a knock at the centre door.*)

PAI-LU (*without turning her head*): Come in.
(*Fu-sheng comes in, stifling a yawn.*)
PAI-LU (*still not turning*): How's it going, Yueh-ting?
FU-SHENG: Miss.
PAI-LU (*turning*): Oh, it's you.
FU-SHENG: Mr. Pan sent me over to tell you he won't be coming after all.
PAI-LU: I see.
FU-SHENG: He says he doesn't think he'll be able to come the next few days, either.
PAI-LU: I know.
FU-SHENG: He told me to tell you to look after yourself, and he said you must always be careful what you're doing, and take care of yourself. He said—
PAI-LU: I understand. He won't be able to come any more.
FU-SHENG: That's right. But Miss, why must you go and offend a wealthy man like Mr. Pan? . . . Isn't it enough to have offended Mr. Chin, without—
PAI-LU (*shaking her head*): You don't understand. I haven't offended him.
FU-SHENG: But when I gave him the bills that you owe a minute ago, just casually like, all he did was to shake his head and sigh, and he went off without saying a word.
PAI-LU: Why did you have to go showing him my bills again?
FU-SHENG: But Miss, they've got to be paid today for sure. They say they won't take any excuses this time. It comes to two thousand five hundred dollars all told, and they won't take a penny less. And you don't want to ruin your reputation by having a long row with them and making a scandal! If you can't find some way of getting the money out of Mr. Pan, where do you think it's coming from? Do you think it's going to drop out of the sky?
PAI-LU: I'll find a way somehow.

FU-SHENG: Oh well, it's up to you to do what you can in the next few hours. I've done all I can; I can't keep them at bay for you any longer.

PAI-LU (*picking up the bottle of sleeping-tablets and gripping it tightly in her hand*): All right, you can go now.

(*Just as Fu-sheng is going out through the centre door, there is a loud knocking on the door to the left and a voice shouting "Open the door, open up!" Fu-sheng comes back into the room and goes over to the door. When he opens it, Georgy Chang bursts in, his face bathed in perspiration.*)

GEORGY (*distraught*): Here, what had you got the door locked for?

FU-SHENG (*smiling*): It wasn't locked. Why should it be?

GEORGY (*clutching his heart*): I had a horrible dream, Pai-lu. It was horrible, ghastly! *C'était affreux! Affreux!* I dreamed the building was full of devils, jumping and leaping all over the place, on the stairs, in the dining-room, on the beds, under the armchairs, on top of the tables, all gnawing at living heads, living arms, living thighs, laughing and gibbering, throwing human skulls back and forth, croaking and snarling. Suddenly there was a great crash and the whole building collapsed, with you crushed beneath it, and me crushed beneath it, and a whole lot of other people crushed beneath it. . . .

(*Fu-sheng goes out through the centre door.*)

PAI-LU (*paying no attention to what he is saying*): I thought you'd gone.

GEORGY: Well, you wouldn't be able to see me here now if I had, now would you! I fell asleep in an armchair in the corner in there.

PAI-LU: You've been overdoing the drinks again.

GEORGY: Yes, I don't deny it. I had a drop too much and it upset my nerves. That's what made me have this nightmare. (*Yawning*) I'm tired. I'll be getting home now. Oh, yes (*suddenly becoming animated*), I've got something to tell you —

PAI-LU: No, wait a moment, there's something I want you to do for me.

GEORGY: Go ahead. Anything you like.

PAI-LU: Someone . . . wants . . . wants me to lend them three thousand dollars.

GEORGY: Oh?

PAI-LU: But just at the moment I can't lay my hands on as much as that for them.

GEORGY: I see.

PAI-LU: Georgy, couldn't you find three thousand dollars for me, to lend this person?

GEORGY: Well . . . er . . . of course . . . that's rather a different matter. I've always been a generous man. Though it depends who's involved. No, I can't lend money to your friend, because . . . because I'm jealous of him, whoever he is. Though of course if it was someone as attractive as yourself who wanted to borrow such a paltry sum for their own use, then I wouldn't hesitate for a moment.

PAI-LU (*reluctantly*): All right, then: let's pretend I'm borrowing it from you myself.

GEORGY: You? Lulu borrow money from me? Borrow money from Georgy Chang?

PAI-LU: Yes, why not?

GEORGY: No, no, I refuse to believe that. Lulu borrow a miserable sum like that? *Ah non,* I refuse to believe that! You're pulling my leg. (*Laughing aloud*) You'll be the death of me. Lulu borrowing money from me, and borrowing such a paltry sum! Oh, my little Lulu, you're a clever girl, you've a wonderful sense of humour. There's not another girl in the world as clever as you. Ah well, I'll say good-bye now. (*He picks up his hat.*)

PAI-LU: Goodbye, then. (*With a faint smile*) You're no fool, either.

GEORGY: Thanks for the compliment! (*Going to the door*) Oh, yes, before I forget, there's something I want to tell you. I couldn't hold out any longer, so I've accepted her after all. I'm thinking — we're thinking of getting married tomorrow. But I told her I must have you as a bridesmaid.

PAI-LU: You want me for a bridesmaid?

GEORGY: Of course you. It would be impossible to find anyone as good.

PAI-LU: All right, then. Well, goodbye.

GEORGY: Goodbye. So it's agreed. *Bonne nuit!* — I mean: good morning, my little Lulu. (*With a wave of his hand he goes out through the centre door.*)

(*The glow of morning gradually filters in through the window, and the first glint of sunlight begins to touch the rooftops. Pai-lu closes the door and goes and sits down at the table in the centre. After staring vacantly in front of her for a moment she gets up and walks up and down a few steps, surveying the room with the regret of parting. Then she goes to the little occasional table by the sofa, picks up a bottle and pours herself a drink. She takes several large gulps, then stands by the sofa lost in thought.*)

(*The centre door creaks open and Fu-sheng comes in.*)

PAI-LU (*in a low, strained voice*): What do you want?

FU-SHENG: Aren't you going to bed yet? It's light, and the sun's already up.

PAI-LU: Yes, I know.

FU-SHENG: Shall I get you a drink of bean-milk before you go to bed?

PAI-LU: No, don't bother. You needn't stay.

FU-SHENG (*taking a bundle of bills out of his pocket*): Er — Miss, these are the bills that have got to be paid today. I'll — I'll leave them here, so that you can check them. (*He puts the bills on the centre table.*)

PAI-LU: All right, leave them there, then.

FU-SHENG: Nothing more you require?

(Pai-lu shakes her head.)

(Fu-sheng turns his back on Pai-lu and yawns wearily, then leaves by the centre door.)

(Pai-lu finishes the drink and puts down the glass. She goes to the centre table and slowly goes through the bills, tossing each one on the floor when she has looked at it, until the floor by the table is littered with them.)

PAI-LU *(heaving a sigh)*: Yes.

(She picks up the sleeping-tablets from the table and goes over to the armchair under the window. She removes the stopper and begins tipping out the tablets one or two at a time, then suddenly stops undecided and collapses weakly in the armchair, where she sits for a moment staring blankly in front of her. She looks up and catches sight of her reflection in the dressing-mirror on the door of the wardrobe to the left of the armchair. She stands up and goes over to the mirror.)

PAI-LU *(she turns this way and that as she examines the beautiful woman in the mirror, then slowly turns to face her squarely. She shakes her head and sighs. Bleakly)*: Not what you'd call unattractive, really. *(After a pause)* You couldn't call her old. Yet. . . . *(She heaves a long sigh. Unable to bear the sight any longer, she paces slowly back to the centre table and begins counting out the tablets from the bottle, a faint smile on her lips, pitying herself with immense warm-heartedness yet at the same time with the anguish of loneliness.)* One, two, three, four, five, six, seven, eight, nine, ten. *(Holding the ten small objects tightly in her hand, she tosses the empty bottle with a crash into a spittoon. She lays her arm on the table and stretches it out to its full length, looking in front of her, nodding her head slightly and speaking sadly.)* So — young, and — so — beautiful, so — *(Silent tears trickle down her cheeks. She takes a firm hold of her-*

self and stands up. She picks up a teacup, turns her head away, and determinedly swallows the tablets in two gulps.)

(A shaft of sunlight now edges into the room and falls on the littered floor. The sky is now brilliant, and outside the window the labourers working on the foundations of the new building have already assembled and now, with the sun on their faces, they are coming closer and closer with grave, rhythmical tread, their "hung-hung-yow, hung-hung-yow" sounding in the distance. Team by team the wooden rammers thud into the earth, and the heavy stone rammers fall with a muffled echo; the heavy "hung-hung-yow, hung-hung-yow" is followed by the soldier-like even tramp of the labourers at their work. They have not yet begun singing their pile-driving song.)

PAI-LU *(tossing the cup aside, her attention held by the sound of the wooden rammers outside, she squares her shoulders and goes to the window. She draws back the curtains and the sunlight falls on her face as she looks out, speaking in a low voice):* "The sun is risen, and the darkness is left behind." *(She takes a breath of the cool morning air, shivers, and looks round.)* "But the sun is not for us, for we shall be asleep." *(Suddenly she switches off the light and draws the curtains to again, so that the room is plunged in darkness, except for a shaft or two of sunlight quivering through the gap between the curtains. She thumps her chest as if she feels pain or constriction there. She picks up the copy of* Sunrise *from the sofa, then lies down on the sofa, preparing to read quietly. . . .)*

(Far, far away the faint voices of the labourers begin a pile-driving song — the Chou Hao. But we cannot make out the words.)

TA-SHENG'S VOICE *(outside):* Chu-chun! Chu-chun! *(The voice approaches the door.)*

(Pai-lu hurriedly puts the book down, stands up, and goes to the door. Realizing who it is, she looks all round, then at once collects up the bills on the table, screws them into a ball in her hand, then picks up the book and hurries into the room on the right, her footsteps already showing signs of heaviness. She closes the door behind her and locks it.)

TA-SHENG'S VOICE *(subdued)*: Chu-chun! Chu-chun! Is there someone with you? Chu-chun!, Chu-chun! I'm leaving now! *(Getting no reply)* I'm coming in, then, Chu-chun.

(The twittering of a sparrow is heard outside the window.)

(Ta-sheng pushes open the door and comes in.)

TA-SHENG *(looking around the room)*: Chu-chun! I say — *(Suddenly realizing how dark it is in the room, he goes to the window and pulls the curtains open again. Sunlight floods in, and with it the twittering of birds.)* I can't understand you not letting the sun in. *(Going to the door of the bedroom on the left)* Listen while I tell you something, Chu-chun. If you go on living like this you'll be digging your own grave. Now listen, why not go with me after all, instead of tying yourself to these people? Now what about it? Look *(pointing out of the window)*, the sun's shining, it's spring.

(The singing of the labourers is now coming nearer. They are singing: "The sun comes up from the east; the sky is a great red glow. . . .")

TA-SHENG *(knocking on the door)*: Listen! Listen! *(Rapturous)* The sun is shining, the sun is on their faces. Come with me, together we can achieve something. We can fight the Mr. Chins, we can — *(Realizing that he is going to be ignored)* Chu-chun, why won't you take any notice of me? *(Tapping on the door)* Why won't you — *(Turning away with a sigh)* You're too clever.

You know better than to be a fool. (*Suddenly pulling himself together*) All right, then, I'll go. Good-bye.

(*Still getting no reply from the other room, he turns his head to listen to the pile-driving song outside the window, then goes out through the centre door, his head held high and the sun on his face.*)

(*The room is flooded with the sunlight streaming in through the window, and outside everything is dazzlingly bright.*)

(*Lusty and strong, the labourers' voices are chorusing the* Chou Hao: *"The sun comes up from the east; the sky is a great red glow! If we want rice to eat we must bend our backs in toil!"*)

(*The heavy stone rammers thud steadily into the earth with a sound that comes to the audience' ears as that of a great surge of life advancing in a mighty tide, flooding the whole universe with its power.*)

(*The light begins to fade inside the room, but outside it shines brighter still.*)

— *THE CURTAIN SLOWLY FALLS* —

About the Author

Tsao Yu is the pen-name of Wan Chia-pao. He was born in 1910 in Chienchiang County in the province of Hupeh and educated at the Nankai Secondary School in Tientsin and Tsinghua University in Peking. It was during his school days that his passionate interest in drama developed. He not only acted and directed but also wrote plays. After graduation he stayed on at the university as a research student; later, he taught in the National Drama Institute and Futan University. In 1945 he went on a lecture tour in the United States. On his return the following year he became a script-writer and film director at the Wenhua Studios in Shanghai.

After liberation, he took part in the World Peace Congress held in Czechoslovakia in 1949. He is at present Vice-President of the Central Theatrical Institute and Director of the Peking People's Art Theatre. He is also a deputy to the National People's Congress, to which he was elected in 1954 and 1959.

His other plays than *Sunrise* include *Thunderstorm* (1933), *Wilderness* (1936), *Transformation* (1940), *Peking Man* (1941), *The Family* (adapted from Pa Chin's novel of the same title in 1941) and *Bright Skies* (1954).

日　　出

曹禺　著

巴恩斯　譯

*

外文出版社出版（北京）

1960年7月第一版

編号：（英）10050—423

00250